Beyond tchblade

Beyond the Cross and the Switchblade

by

DAVID WILKERSON

WITH A FOREWORD BY
JOHN AND ELIZABETH SHERRILL

HODDER AND STOUGHTON
LONDON SYDNEY AUCKLAND TORONTO

ISBN 0 340 21260 8

Published by Hodder and Stoughton, a division of Hodder and Stoughton
Ltd, Mill Road, Dunton Green, Sevenoaks, Kent TN13 2YA. Editorial
Office: 47 Bedford Square, London WC1B 3DP.

Printed in Great Britain by Cox & Wyman Ltd, Reading.

Contents

Foreword

PEOPLE ARE CONSTANTLY asking us what's happened to David Wilkerson since we wrote *The Cross and the Switchblade* together.

We've kept up regularly with Dave and Gwen, meeting occasionally to talk over problems with the movie, or the latest developments in their work. We followed their moves from Staten Island to Massapequa, Long Island, and eventually to Dallas, Texas. In each move one thing has remained constant: Dave and Gwen still like to live simply. Shortly after they settled in Dallas, for instance, they needed a new car. Gwen has always dreamed of driving a luxury automobile (as who hasn't!). When an unexpected gift came in, designated for their personal use, Dave made a down-payment on a Mark IV.

The first day Gwen was in ecstasies. But on the second day she had to drive it into the church parking lot. "It looked so ridiculous there," she told us. "The glamour just evaporated. Who were the Wilkersons to be driving a Mark IV!" Within a week she had traded in her dream for a family station wagon. We drove in that car recently. It rattles. But there is something 'right' about it, just as there is about Dave and Gwen themselves.

If the parents haven't changed much, the kids of course are unrecognisable:

Debbie, a pre-schooler when we first knew the family, is 20 years old, presently working full time with Teen Challenge in Holland.

Bonnie is now 18, a student at Evangel College in Springfield, Missouri. She wants to be a Christian writer.

Gary, born in Pennsylvania while Dave was preaching on the New York City sidewalks, is 15 today and taller than his dad. He plans to attend a Bible College to prepare for the ministry.

Greg wasn't even born when we worked on the book. Eight years old now, he's finally abandoned the idea of growing up to be a candy salesman and decided instead to be a 'preacher like my daddy'.

Not all the news in the Wilkerson family has been good, however. Gwen, for example, has had a prolonged bout with cancer. And David's work has had setbacks, some of them occasioned by his own mistakes.

So when David asked us what he should put into a book that would bring people up to date, we had three suggestions.

First, he should include follow-up stories of people mentioned in *The Cross and the Switchblade* – people, we know from our mail, about whom readers continue to be concerned.

And then he should talk about what has happened to his work since — and partly because of — the publication of the book. He should tell about the movie, and Pat Boone's role in making it. He should talk freely, we believed, about the book's financial difficulties. Paradoxically although the book eventually sold 11,000,000 copies and the movie played to packed houses, both publisher and film producer reported such serious money problems that they were having trouble paying their bills. We thought he should tell what this meant to him and Gwen.

But most important, perhaps, we hoped that Dave would talk about his mistakes, and what he has learned about walking in the Spirit since the publication of *The Cross and the Switchblade*. This should be a book about people, yes. But it should be more than that. It should also include in each chapter some account of the spiritual adventure that has been increasingly a part of his and Gwen's life together.

Here is Dave Wilkerson, 1974. *Beyond the Cross and the Switchblade* fulfils every one of our expectations about it. More than that it offers guidance and direction for each of us seeking to know God's will in the quarter-century ahead.

JOHN AND ELIZABETH SHERRILL

I

The Trysting Place

Do you have a secret place where you can count on meeting the Lord?

IT IS JULY 1972 and the flight across the Atlantic has been uneventful. Not even a hijack attempt. Yet all twelve of us from our team at World Challenge, based in Dallas, Texas, are elated. For we are coming home.

We had been in Europe for four weeks, holding twenty different one-night rallies during that time. How often we praised the Lord for a four-day boat trip up the Rhine during that time: else I frankly don't think we would have found the strength we needed. The crowds which turned out were much larger than we had anticipated: eight, ten, twelve thousand people at a time. They had all come to hear the 'skinny country preacher' David Wilkerson, whose story they all seemed to have read in *The Cross and the Switchblade*. Except for Helsinki, Finland, where students had been told that I was a CIA agent sent to propagandise Europe into accepting Mr. Nixon's viewpoint about the war in Vietnam — except for this one situation, the crowds were welcoming, hundreds upon hundreds of young people gave their lives to the Lord and in general we had a feeling of success behind us. Even when Gwen suddenly doubled up with pain and had to be taken off the aeroplane on a stretcher, we knew victory. For we ignored the whispering voice that said, 'This is Gwen's cancer coming back.' Instead we prayed for an immediate healing. Gwen was out of the hospital the next day, feeling fine.

I too had scored a small victory over my fear of flying. At least I got aboard; that was something! How I had to struggle against my fear on this trip. Everyone suffered with me as my palms began to sweat before take-off and as my knuckles turned white from gripping the seat arm so tightly.

Yet somehow I managed to get that huge 747 all the way across the Atlantic and now here we were at last circling Kennedy.

There below was New York, with its eight million people, its impossible crowding, its filth, its ghettoes, its black-against-Puerto Rican; Jew-against-WASP. Quite a contrast to Holland, Switzerland, Norway, Finland, where government seems to have taken so much of the risk out of life: no slums there to speak of, no worries about medical expenses, no problems of homeless old age.

We certainly couldn't say that about America. The country we were coming back to was festering with problems. Yet we knew that this was where we belonged. We had been called to work here, with people from slum and suburb alike, people who are hurting.

Coming in from the airport, Gwen and I rode with Edgar Palser, the pastor of our new church home in Dallas. Edgar and his wife Sarah had gone to Europe with us. They had spent very little time in New York and were goggle-eyed as we came off the expressway and plunged into the same cancer we had been looking at an hour before from the window of the 747.

Edgar and Sarah did not know how excited I was to be

coming back to New York. Over the years I have developed a habit of visiting what I call my Trysting Places, special rendezvous points where in the past I have met the Lord and where I return in time of need, confident that I will find Him there again. There is a strange power in *place*. This must be one of the main reasons the Bible gives such an important role to altars and sanctuaries and special mountains. For by instinct we are drawn back to the place where we once met God, trusting that there again we can keep our tryst.

In a strange way a particular house in Bedford-Stuyvesant, Brooklyn, was for me just such a Trysting Place. Odd that I could have a Trysting Place in Bedford-Stuyvesant, where they say there are more murders per square foot than any other place in the world. But I had met the Lord many times in this cesspool. I had met Him as we stood together beside a junkie, screaming as he tried to come off heroin; or as we looked together into the eyes of a frightened black boy who dared not leave his one square block because this was his turf; or into the face of a girl who had just knelt on a street corner to give her life away.

Now I knew that I needed to come back to Bedford-Stuyvesant as a Trysting Place because of a problem I was facing. Over the years our work had taken us further and further from the city of New York itself. Our parish became, in time, not one city but the whole country, city and suburb, farm and village. Because it was more centrally located we had even moved our headquarters to Dallas, Texas. Teen Challenge in New York was now only one part of my overall work with World Challenge.

Yet I was still concerned for New York. Never a day passed without deep intercession for her. Just a few minutes ago, as we were coming into Kennedy and I looked down at the sprawling ugliness below me, I found myself praying that the Lord meet me again in our old Trysting Place with a word of encouragement ... or with a word of correction ... about the move we had made out into a larger parish. 'What about the city, Lord?' I had said. 'What about New York? I believe I heard You tell me to leave the work here to others now. But I would like a fresh word.'

Now as Gwen and I rode along with Edgar and Sarah, I tried to tell them about New York, pointing out landmarks that were so well known to me from my days of working the streets of Brooklyn. There was Public School #67 in the Fort Greene Projects where I had first preached to Nicky and Israel. Edgar's bright eyes looked around inquiringly. Places he knew well from the book sprang alive before him. I grew silent looking at them too.

Edgar interrupted my reverie, 'David,' he said, 'before I left on this trip I asked the Lord to show me a project where our church could help. I mean, here you are with the work in New York thriving financially ...' (I wanted to chuckle at that one, but I didn't say anything.) '... so, if you'll pardon me, I don't think we should try to help Teen Challenge. We want another work. I prayed that the Lord would show me what He had in mind.'

So we didn't spend too much time at Teen Challenge. Gwen and I just took Edgar and Sarah on a short tour of 416 Clinton Avenue, where everything began, showing them the rooms where to this day kids go through the agony of withdrawal. We showed them the neighbouring buildings the Lord had given us for our work since the finishing of *The Cross and the Switchblade*. I took them by to meet my brother Don who runs things in the New

York area, and my mother who still has her work among young people in Greenwich Village, where she is known as the 'Village Square'. And finally we visited the room where we had read the letter from Clement Stone with the great news that he was going to make a grant of money to help us launch our work nation-wide.

I asked Edgar if there were something else he would like to see.

'Yes. Can we visit one of the places where people have been shooting up,' Edgar said.

I knew right away where we should go. The four of us got in the car and went back towards Second Avenue. While we were still driving along I said:

'Take out your wallet, Edgar. Our wallets and Sarah's and Gwen's purses go under the seat.' The Palsers looked at me, puzzled. 'There's no use asking for trouble,' I said.

We got out, locked the car carefully and started down Second Avenue. 'You walk between us,' I said to Sarah and Gwen, wondering how I could say what I needed to say without sounding dramatic. 'Try to pretend you are a building inspector or something. You're not down here slumming. The chances are we'll be left alone.'

I made these comments because on more than one occasion people coming to Bedford-Stuyvesant to walk the streets I had walked found themselves mugged. We continued on down this familiar avenue until we came to a building very familiar to me. There I stopped.

'This is a place where I saw kids shooting up,' I said.

And there standing by a heap of garbage piled up in front of the tenement, I told the Palsers about the time I had come across five boys from the street gangs here. They were lolling around, leaning against this very fence, when up I came, the greenhorn preacher. One boy recognised me from the papers. My picture had been spread over the tabloids because I had tried to help some gang members and got myself in trouble with the law. 'Ha, here's the Preach who got his self kicked out of court,' one of the boys said.

The others seemed a little interested. They stood slightly more at attention and commented about the Bible I was carrying. 'You got something in there for us, Preach?' And I started to talk to them. I told them the very simple story of how they were loved: just as they were. Right then, right there.

But the boys were falling asleep. Their eyes closed and they seemed bored. It got me angry. I took a big risk. I shook one of them sharply on the shoulder. 'What's the trouble, how come you're going to sleep?'

'Man, don't you know? We're junkies.'

'Shut up, Shorty,' one of the boys said.

'Don't worry,' Shorty said. 'He ain't no Narco. He's a Hallelujah Man.'

So we got to talking. In the end Shorty and his friends offered to let me go on a little trip with them: I could watch them shooting if I wanted. Well, I didn't want. In the first place I would be breaking the law, but far more important than that, I would be watching a young boy do something which could kill him. On the other hand if I was ever to reach these kids I would have to find out what their lives were like.

So in the end I agreed. We went inside the urine-smelling, dark hallways and climbed six floors to the roof, kicked open a broken door. There, behind a parapet, Shorty picked up an old Coca-Cola bottle that was nearly full of dirty water. He took out his works, a metal bottle cap and a match, a piece of rubber tubing and a syringe. He dipped the needle in the filthy water.

'What are you doing that for?' I asked.

'I'm sterilising the needle, Man.'

Shorty took a glassine bag of white powder out of his hatband and poured it into the bottle cap, heated the mixture, drew it into the needle, wrapped the tubing around his arm until his vein swelled and then injected directly into the swollen vein.

Shorty's eyes were yellow, his skin yellow. He was jaundiced. That infected needle, pulled out of his vein, was immediately plunged again into the vein of the next boy. And then into the vein of another. As a third youngster shot up, I fainted.

The next thing I knew someone was slapping my face. 'What's the matter, Preach, you chicken?' I sat up. I realised where I was and what was happening.

'Chicken, yeah. Yeah, I'm chicken. Shorty's got jaundice, can't you see? With that needle all of you are going to get hepatitis.'

'That's not why you passed out, Man. You just couldn't take the sight of the shooting gallery. Don't you know, hepatitis ain't no scare. There's no hope for us except an O.D.'

There on the rooftop, squatting behind a parapet in the tar and dirt, I made a clearcut prayer, 'Lord, I promise You that I will never again go out preaching the words of salvation until I can prove that there is help right here, in this very situation. Either we really have something to say or we don't. Show me, Lord Jesus. Show me.'

That had all been so long ago. Fifteen years. The work with addicts had grown out of that prayer. Often, in times of despair I would come back to this Trysting Place for refreshment. Now on this hot summer day, standing in front of the same building with Edgar and Sarah Palser, Gwen and I made our way up the stone steps into the foyer of the decrepit ghetto building. It seemed that nothing at all had changed. There was still the smell of urine. Windows were still broken. There was still the sticky substance on the walls where kids had shaken pop bottles and squirted them. There were still the obscenities scrawled on the woodwork. There were still the harsh arguing behind closed and, doubtless, triple-locked doors.

We made our way up the six flights of stairs, panting in the heat. There was the same roofwell, the same broken door. We kicked it open and stood at the same sheltered place behind the parapet where Shorty and his friends had 'sterilised' their needle in a Coca-Cola bottle full of dirty water. We were in the midst of reviewing the prayer I had made so long ago in this odd Trysting Place, where I had once asked for help from the Lord. All of a sudden there was a noise behind us and out of the stairwell appeared a black man.

'What are you people doing on my roof?'

His question wasn't particularly hostile, just doubtful and curious. I introduced myself, my wife and the Palsers and I told him how I had committed my own life to working with kids in trouble on this same rooftop fifteen years earlier.

'You don't mean you're the guy from Teen Challenge?' the big man said.

'This is where it all started.'

'In my building? What do you know. I am the landlord.' And then he proceeded to tell us how he was trying to act out the gospel in his own special way by buying up old buildings and turning them into decent homes. 'Mostly it don't work,' the landlord added. 'But I do have one good thing going. Come on and I'll show you.'

The bulky man worked his way down the dirty stairs. On the way, two devastating little experiences told us what the landlord meant when he said his experiment wasn't working. As we were passing a window a large bag of garbage went sailing by. It plopped into the courtyard below. 'There!' said the landlord, 'I can't even *hire* these people to clean up.' And worse: as we were coming on to the third floor we met two black kids. They must have been ten or twelve years old. They were standing in the corner with their sleeves rolled up, and they were jabbing toothpicks at their veins, as if shooting up. When they saw us they started to wobble their heads, like they were jiving.

'Get out you two!' the landlord shouted. He turned to us apologetically. 'See what I mean? What can I do? They are trying to be like their big brothers.'

I could hear stifled sobs coming from Edgar's wife as we continued to follow our guide down into the basement.

In order to get to the basement of this ghetto house, we had first to go outside, walk around the cast-iron fence and work our way down a set of stone steps. The first thing I noticed was how scrubbed and clean the steps were. Our host then knocked on the basement door and shortly there appeared the face of a middle-aged Puerto Rican.

'Fernando,' called the landlord, 'can we come in?'
The Puerto Rican opened his door wide and stood back.

'Praise the Lord!' he said, as we moved in. I knew instantly that I was in a holy place. There were six cots in the room. Ceiling tiles had been cemented over the old plaster: the tiles had been put in crooked. The walls were freshly painted: it was a very amateur job. Hand-lettered signs were plastered on the walls, with the words running crooked: one said, 'Don't fool yourself! You're not all alone.' There was something about the homemade quality of the room that made me know that this was consecrated ground for Fernando and the people, whoever they were, who slept on those cots.

The landlord introduced us and then told us a little of Fernando's story: The man, incredibly, had been a heroin addict for thirty-five years and for most of that time he had been mainlining. I didn't think that was possible! His addiction had cost him his family; his wife left him, his children would have nothing to do with him. It cost him his job, his self-respect, his health. But then one day Fernando stumbled on to one of our Teen Challenge street meetings. Quite literally out of the gutter he turned his life over to God and experienced one of those miracles that always encourage me: Fernando, thirty-five years addicted, was able with God's help to kick his habit. In time Teen Challenge hired him as a handyman. We paid him fifty dollars a week.

'And this is where the story really begins,' said the landlord, smiling at Fernando. 'Man, it was so great. He came to me because he knew I was trying to help my people, and asked if he could have this basement rent-free for three years. So I asked him, Why? And he said he wants to turn the place into a Block Rehabilitation Centre, just specialising in the kids from this one block, see? So I said sure, why not. And Fernando starts to tithe, like. Except it was more ninety per cent for the Lord, ten per cent for himself. And this is what he's done!' The landlord swept his large arm appreciatively around the scruffy room. I saw it with his eyes too, as a place to be treasured.

'Do our people at Teen Challenge know about your work?' I asked him.

'No, I wanted to get it going first. I've brought four kids to the Lord here. They're clean now, and they live here. But I'll tell you the truth, Brother Dave, I sometimes wonder how I'm going to make out. These kids shouldn't go back into their homes. But it's kind of hard feeding four boys, plus myself, getting them some clothes, and bus fare while they are looking for work — all on fifty dollars a week.' I found myself looking into the eyes of Pastor Palser. He gave me a nod. The Lord had answered his prayer for a work in Brooklyn that his church could support.

A little later Edgar and Sarah and Gwen and I were seated again in our automobile. Suddenly I started to laugh. It was a strange healthy, holy laugh such as I had known on only a few occasions in my life. I think it must have been a kind of praising-laugh, for it was mixed with thanksgiving. I didn't try to stifle it. Soon Gwen, Edgar and Sarah joined me. We must have laughed for a full three minutes, merrily, as if living water of joy were being poured through us. We all knew exactly what the experience meant.

'Though I make my bed in hell, thou art there,' quoted Edgar. And we all laughed some more. For that was exactly it. Each of us was certain that this squalid building on Second Avenue with its garbage plopping down in its inner court, with its urine-smelling hallways, and its rooftop which had been used as a place for junkies to meet — incredibly this was a place where God lives.

'Lord, thank You so much for giving us this understanding of the way You work today,' I said. 'Thank You for placing Fernando's work on our hearts. Thank You for answering my question about the move to Dallas. For I see now that You are raising up a second generation of consecrated people in this city. I see now that Your work doesn't depend upon individuals at all. Not me. Not Don or Mother or any of the team at Teen Challenge. This is Your work and You are going to keep on blooming it.'

We took our wallets and purses from underneath the seat, put the car in gear and drove away from Holy Ground.

So that was one visit to one Trysting Place, at a time when I needed it desperately. I went back to Dallas encouraged and confident that the shift in our work to a more national character really had been guided. Edgar and his wife took Fernando's work as a part of their missionary prayer concern. The landlord took courage and did stay on at the building.

I frankly don't know what I would have done since completing *The Cross and the Switchblade* without Trysting Places, especially at turning points in life. I could so easily understand why Jacob knelt at Peniel, '. . . for I have seen God face to face, and my life is preserved' (Genesis 32:30), and why Abraham built his altars, '. . . unto the Lord, who appeared unto him' (Genesis 12:7), and why the Psalmist would say, 'I was glad when they said unto me, Let us go into the house of the Lord' (Psalm 122:1).

But usually for me Trysting Places have not been

locations I would share with other people. For me they were likely to be secluded spots, quite private, where I once met the Lord with a specific question in mind. To these places I could always return when life became unbearable. On the way home to Dallas I got to thinking about one of those times.

I was in trouble. But I didn't know it myself.

I really had not dreamed that the publication of *The Cross and the Switchblade* was going to make so much difference in my life.

The book contained an epilogue in which I said, about our work, that the Holy Spirit was in charge here. At that moment in time — late 1964 — such a statement was true and accurate. We were still a peanuts operation. We had to depend utterly on the Lord. Whether we wanted to or not we remained a pretty simple lot.

The appearance of the book changed all of that.

Suddenly I was considered a drug expert. There was a big spread about Teen Challenge and the work we were doing with addicts in *Life Magazine*. There was coverage in *Time*. The *New York Times* and the *Daily News* and *The Post* all did features about us. I was on network television and radio. The speaking invitations came in faster than I could turn them down. I had to have three telephone lines installed in my office to handle all the calls, and four secretaries just to handle the flow of correspondence. People started stopping me on the street to ask me questions. At home we had to go to an unlisted telephone number for the first time in our lives. In short, I was no longer a private person.

And then one day — it was in the summer of 1968, four years after the book came out — I was quite literally running between the old building at 416 Clinton Avenue and the new headquarters building we had purchased down the street, 444 Clinton Avenue.

Suddenly, a Chinese man was standing in my way. I had not seen the man coming. Anyway there he was now, right in my path. I tried to move to the left and he moved to block me. I tried to move the other way and he moved too. Finally I stopped. The weather was very hot, humid and I was impatient.

'Excuse me.' I tried to get around him again only to be blocked one more time. So I had to stop.

'You are David Wilkerson,' the man said. It was a statement, not a question. He looked at me out of narrow, quiet eyes, a peace telling me I had to stand still. 'I am a man of God,' the Chinese said in immaculate English, 'and I live in Hongkong. I have been sent by the Lord to speak to you. My message is very simple. You are depending too much on David Wilkerson. You are not depending on the Spirit. You have lost simplicity.'

Well, that really did it. That really blew my mind. How dare this little Chinese stop me on my way to an important interview. Didn't he know that I was preaching to 6,000 people a week, that my drug rehabilitation work had spread from this centre to the suburbs and from there out into the grassroots of the country? I didn't say it in so many words, but I'm sure every note, every tone spelled out what I really meant: 'How dare you stop this important man, David Wilkerson?'

Well, the Chinese was hurt, I could tell that. His eyes filled with tears. 'I'm not worrying for myself, David. I'm crying for you. I would not have made you angry for the world. I know that you have been used of the Lord. Still, I must obey. I was told to speak to you. That I had to do.'

And the little man walked past me. I stood there on the sidewalk for a while, perspiring, wondering where he had learned his very good English, then I shrugged and ran quickly to my appointment, satisfied that this could not have been of the Lord. The Lord would not reprove me with hurt this way. The Lord was gentle.

And I said as much to Gwen that night. 'That was pretty silly, wasn't it? That Chinese telling me I had lost my simplicity.'

'Silly?' Gwen said. 'No.'

Now Gwen was never one to scold. However, neither was I able to fool her. I might turn aside the mysterious Chinese, but when Gwen herself added approval to his thoughts, I had to listen carefully. Had we indeed lost our simplicity?

Our own standard of living had not changed greatly since Phillipsburg days, before we moved to New York, but we did own a comfortable split-level house and drove a comfortable car. Even my prayer-room was comfortable: I had made a retreat-room out of a portion of our garage. And it was there that I went now, trying to think about this question of simplicity.

After a while I became restless and took Gwen to a little Italian restaurant near home where we often went when we needed to talk. We just sat there and held hands and nibbled on antipasto and chatted.

'Of course, the Lord does raise up *voices*, sometimes,' Gwen said. 'Voices we don't want to hear. Prophets who are sent with a word from the Lord.'

'Do you think our Chinese was one of these?'

'How can I say, David? As the old song says, God works in mysterious ways.'

By the end of our antipasto I was saying to Gwen,

'Well, I guess I'll have to go for a little trip. I've got to find a Trysting Place.'

And so it was that next day I cancelled all appointments and set out to make a pilgrimage to an old Trysting Place. I left Gwen and the kids, the work at 416 Clinton Avenue and headed back across George Washington Bridge, reversing the trip Miles Hoover and I had made into New York so many years ago. I headed first of all for Barnesboro, Pennsylvania, wondering if perhaps God's Trysting Place for me were here in childhood settings. I drove past the high school where I had faced down our high school bully and first learned the practical meaning of the phrase, 'Not by might, nor by power, but by My Spirit, saith the Lord of Hosts.' But at the high school I had no inclination to stop.

So I drove out to Old Baldy hill. The place brought back memories all right. Below, I could see the country road leading away from Barnesboro towards the town of Cherry Tree; it was still the same ever-thinning road disappearing into the distance. I used to sit here as a boy, wondering where that road went and what was over those hills. It was here that I used to indulge in fantasies about enemy pilots attacking the United States. There were fierce dog fights above Barnesboro which I watched with my child's eye. And of course both good guys and bad guys crashed into the Pennsylvania hills, burning alive in fireballs, like the fires of hell my father preached about from his pulpit.

'But Old Baldy's not where You want me to go, Lord,' I said. 'You're pulling me someplace else. So let's go.'

I squeezed back into my automobile and headed towards Philipsburg.

I really do think I expected Philipsburg, where I had my

first pastorate, to have changed since I left it years earlier. But as far as I could see the town had not changed an iota. It was still a farmer's burg. It still had just the one factory in it, fabricating cheap clothes for men. And there, still there, was the little church. As I walked past I tagged up on a famous spot, the home plate where Lou Gehrig had once played ball.

No one was around so I stepped into the church, walked down the aisle and took my old place behind the pulpit. In my mind's eye I could see exactly where all of my parishioners sat. There was Brothers Meyers. There was Brother Peters. It would all be the same. I could even imagine our neighbour across the way calling out to us again please to be quiet, we were disturbing her peace.

But it wasn't here either, my Trysting Place.

And then I knew where it was.

How could I have missed! Albert Hill, of course. I got in my car and zipped up to the height, remembering how often I had made this drive in my old two-toned Chevy. I fully expected Albert Hill to be subdivided or filled with trailers or some such. But it too was just the same. I got out of the car, went over to the rock where I always sat and looked out over Philipsburg. The church was down below and I could see the backyard where on so many occasions we drank lemonade with the parishioners.

'That was a *simple* life, Lord. Is this the simplicity You are talking to me about? I'm not sure. Do You want us to stay in our back yards where it is safe and simple, and smooth?'

I had brought along my Bible. My very special Bible. The one I took with me into the court house that day years ago when the Michael Farmer trial began. As I picked it up now, I could still see the faces of the seven boys accused of the murder of a crippled child. I could almost feel the weight of the Bible as I carried it down the aisle to try to speak to the judge at the trial. This was the Bible the press corps persuaded me to hold up while they took pictures which made me look like some sort of country fanatic.

What memories. For years I kept notes in the margins of this Bible. I had misplaced it once, only to have it fall in the hands of a young man who kept it overnight and then returned it with the comment, 'David, I have to confess, I have been reading these marginal notes. You know what they say to me? They give me the picture of a soul in ecstasy and in torment, both.' He had been right about that.

I opened the Bible now and started to read the margin notes and the text that went against them, beginning right in Genesis:

'God grieves. He repents. He rejoices.'

'And it repented the Lord that he had made man on the earth, and it grieved him at his heart.'

—Genesis 6:6

'God demands respect from everyone for His promises.'

'Then Sarah denied, saying, I laughed not for she was afraid. And he said, Nay; but thou didst laugh.'

—Genesis 18:15

'The most important sentence in any language is, "The Lord was with him."'

'But the Lord was with Joseph, and shewed him mercy, and gave him favor in the sight of the keeper of the prison.'

—Genesis 39:21

What did this all have to do with my question? The Chinese man had said I was moving away from simplicity. What kind of simplicity had I known, earlier in life, that the Lord wanted me to retain? Was it a simplicity of *life style*? I had moved from the physically simple life of Philipsburg to the more comfortable life of the suburbs. Was that it? No, probably not. It went deeper. Back in the early days when I first started working with gang members and dope addicts, I had a simplicity that went beyond life style. It was a simplicity of faith.

'Lord there You are! You've showed it to me. This is what You want me to have. You want me to get myself out of the way, to depend absolutely upon You. My life may become complex but my faith should always stay just that simple. I've been leaning on myself and not Your Word.'

I jumped up and clapped my hands and danced as I skipped towards the automobile.

I sang much of the way back to New York. For I saw quite clearly that the Lord had indeed led that Chinese man to me. Now I knew what I had to fear: losing my simplicity of faith.

Just before I reached Manhattan, I passed the place where Miles Hoover and I pulled off the road on our first visit to the city, where the Lord encouraged us to go on. I backed up and got out of the car and walked up the hill.

Yes, it was the some place all right. There were the two trees and there was the gasoline station down the road and there was the guard rail and the pullout. It gave me a feeling of coming full circle.

'Thank You, Lord, for what You did for me on Albert Hill. Let me never again doubt the value of a Trysting

Place. Let me never again lean upon myself. Let me lean, instead, upon You.'

Very shortly I was to learn that dependence upon the Lord extended past what I had imagined. I was trusting Him more now in my personal life. But what about trusting Him too in the lives of others?

2

Holy Ghost Timing

When you're worried about family and friends, how much confidence do you have in. . .

I DO THINK IT IS harder to trust God in the lives of people you love than it is to trust on your own behalf. It took me years to discover the premier lesson that God has a timing all His own, and that I must not be impatient when His timing doesn't coincide with mine.

In those years after I came to New York as what the papers called the 'skinny country preacher' trying to reach the boys accused of murdering Michael Farmer, there was one puzzle which kept coming up in my prayers. I had not been allowed to minister to the boys on trial. 'Why, Lord,' I asked, 'did You have me come all the way to New York with these boys, and then stop me?'

I suppose I had asked God the question a hundred times.

'Why, Lord, especially, did You not let me see Juan Martinez?'

Of the seven boys brought to trial for beating Michael to death three were released and four were given sentences of from twenty years to life. I tried to get permission from the court to visit the jailed boys, but could not even obtain their prison addresses, much less their home addresses. The name of one special boy, Juan Martinez, kept coming to mind in my prayers. Perhaps if I just went through the Martinezes in the phonebook? But when I looked, there were scores of Martinezes listed. I gave up when I had deposited my fortieth dime without a lead. Then I did what I should have done in the first place. I bowed my head.

'Lord,' I prayed, 'I give up. I have reached the limits of my own ideas. Lead me where I must go, for I don't know what to do next.'

And then, incredibly, shortly after that, the Lord told me to stop my car on a particular street at a particular parking place and ask for Juan. I had parked in front of the building where the Martinez family lived.

Coincidence? Had I subconsciously remembered the address from somewhere? I didn't care. I just plunged ahead, got to know the Martinez family and liked them immediately. I learned that Juan was in Elmira prison in upstate New York. I tried several times to make contact with him. Once, in fact, through the Martinez family and a local pastor in Elmira, I actually had permission from the authorities for a visit. But just as I was about to leave New York a phone call came through from the prison. The permission had been rescinded. I was not to come.

At every turn I was being blocked. The only way I could understand it was to say that God did not want me to work with these particular seven boys themselves, but with hundreds of boys *like* them.

Still, even after years had passed, I never quite let go of my wish to see Juan. I prayed for him regularly. At our crusades, when I told the story of the boys, I would include a request for prayer. 'Especially,' I so often said, 'let's pray for Juan Martinez.'

I also noticed an interesting thing about myself. I was ready to accept any invitation to speak in a New York state prison. It didn't matter that my audience usually consisted of only fifty young men instead of the five thousand who often turned out for crusades. I knew my motive: perhaps one day I would run across Juan. It seemed my only hope now. He had been transferred so many times, and each time the trail became fainter.

Then one day still another invitation came from a prison. This time it was from the Auburn State Correctional Facility in Auburn, New York. Their chaplain wrote that shortly after his appointment he had started passing out copies of *The Cross and the Switchblade*. The inmates accepted the books eagerly. Several had asked how they might meet me. And now, the invitation. Of course, once again I accepted.

Auburn has an inmate population of 1,800. The turnout that day wasn't especially good, I imagine 150 people showed up. I preached a very simple sermon and we sang some songs. And then I issued an invitation. I asked the fellows who responded to meet me in their chaplain's office.

Among the prisoners who came there was a studious-looking fairly heavy-set young man. He had a pleasant smile, a dimple on each side of his lips, and an odd habit of poking his finger in my chest as he spoke. Then he threw the bombshell.

'Mr. Wilkerson,' he said, 'I have been waiting for years to meet you. I'm Juan Martinez.'

Well, I just threw my arms around him. 'Juan! I've been waiting for four years to meet you, too!'

We tried to make up for lost time by speaking very

rapidly, one over the other. I told Juan about my many attempts to meet him, and he told me about what had happened since the trial. He told me how all the boys thought I was some kind of nut. A fanatic. The day of the trial they went back to prison laughing. 'Yet I don't believe a single one of us was really laughing, 'cause you were the only dude in New York who was trying to help,' said Juan.

Then he told how he had found a copy of *The Cross and the Switchblade* and that meant a lot to him. 'I got a favour I'd like to ask,' Juan said to me. 'Would you consider praying for me? I want to . . . well . . . I want to change.'

Consider! It had been my dream for years. I pulled Juan aside and asked him to repeat after me what I call the Starting Place Prayer. 'It's really very simple, Juan. You just tell Jesus that you believe He is the Son of God and that you're a sinner and that you would like to turn your life around beginning right now.'

'Yeah,' said Juan. He lowered his eyes and repeated the prayer. When he looked up his eyes were brimming.

'It's the start of a new day, Juan,' I said. 'From now on, nothing can be the same.'

Before I left, Juan and I made arrangements with the chaplain for Juan to have counselling sessions. And also some training in the Bible. Then I gave Juan my name and mailing address; we'd keep in touch.

I was just about ready to step out of the chaplain's office when I heard a hissing sound. I looked up and saw two young black men standing in the hallway, beckoning to me.

'Preach, do you remember us?'

I looked at them closely. How could I possibly remember two boys from the thousands I had met? Yet, they did seem familiar ... 'Was it ... St. Nicholas Arena?' I asked.

'Yeah, it was St. Nick's all right. I'm Raymond, this here's Alan.'

'I remember now, you were with a gang called the Dragons. You wanted to bust up the meeting. You weren't buying.'

'Well, we dig it now, Preach. And we just wanted you to know.'

After the rally at St. Nicholas Arena, Raymond and Alan said, they had gone right on living for dope, violence, sex. For them the crusade had been a washout. Other boys had committed their lives to Jesus but not Raymond, not Alan. On the other hand they could not forget the evening, either. When they were caught in a burglary attempt, brought to trial, sentenced to prison, they found that they were speaking often together of what had happened at St. Nicholas.

'Then, Preach,' Raymond said, 'when the chaplain here passed out copies of that book of yours we found St. Nick's in it. That part of the story was true. It was just like you said. So maybe the rest of the book was true too, about people getting a new start? We began to come to the chaplain's classes and we dig what's going on, Man.'

Just then the guards came to start taking the boys back to their cells. I didn't have a chance to talk further either with Juan or Raymond or Alan. But as I passed through the prison auditorium I noticed a group of five young men huddled on the stage. When they saw me they called,

'Hey, Davie. Come here a minute.'

I turned and walked up the short flight of steps that led to the stage.

'Davie,' one of the boys said, 'maybe you won't believe this but it's true.'

'What's true?'

'Every single one of us here is a drop-out from Teen Challenge.'

There was a chorus of Yes's and That's-right's and then the stories came out, quickly, for the guards were calling. All of the boys were from Brooklyn. All had been involved in drugs. Each had come across our street workers and had agreed to go through the programme at 416 Clinton Avenue. But not one stayed more than three days. For a variety of reasons they dropped out. Either they didn't want to become hallelujah boys, or they couldn't take the discipline, or they couldn't break away from drugs. So they dropped out. And ended up here at Auburn State Correctional Institution.

Just then a guard began to get sharp with the boys for dawdling. So they had to leave. But as they sauntered off the stage they managed to get an *important* thought across to me.

'Davie,' one of the boys said as he walked, 'maybe when we dropped out of your programme, you worried some.' They would never know how much I worried about all our drop-outs. I always prayed for all our boys. Night after night I still kept a rendezvous with the Lord from midnight until two in the morning — I prayed for the kids who seemed to take a step towards the Lord then slid back. 'But don't you see,' the boy in front of me was saying, 'your timing ain't God's.'

'All right,' the guard said.

'Yeah,' said the boy over his shoulder. 'We're all into

Jesus now, David. That's the thing to remember. God's got His own timing.'

Holy Ghost timing? Now there's a new thought.

Holy Ghost timing never fails. In just one day the Lord had preached the same message to me three times. Our timing and the timing of the Holy Ghost were not the same at all. I wanted to plant and harvest all in the day, but the Holy Ghost had a different schedule. I had seen this now in the lives of Juan and Raymond and Alan and the group of five boys.

It was a time for rejoicing. On my way back home I started to sing. I made up a tune to fit the words of Galatians 6:9 '. . . for in due season we shall reap, if we faint not.'

The idea of Holy Ghost Timing was a great encouragement to me. But even as I drove along singing, I realised that I still had a long way to go. For there was always Jerry.

I slowed the car. Yes, Jerry. My own brother. I wondered what bar he was in at that very moment, drinking himself into blank-mindedness. I pulled into the truck lane and moved on slowly. Jerry, Jerry. Where does Holy Ghost timing fit into your life?

It was one thing to have confidence in the Spirit for strangers, quite another to believe for your own family.

'Jesus,' I said, coming to a stop altogether now on the verge of the highway, 'thank You for telling me about Holy Ghost Timing. Take my concern for Jerry now, and replace it with confidence, I pray. Thank You, Lord.'

As if to encourage me about Jerry, the Lord shortly began to show me the different paths He takes in bringing people into His Kingdom in His Timing. For instance, there was Maria.

I remember the first morning I met Maria at the basement door of the 'Clubroom' of the GGI's (Grand Gangsters, Incorporated) on 134th Street in Manhattan. I thought the girl was trying to play a joke on me. She was a storybook figure. She had no shoes on, she was drinking beer from a can, a cigarette hung sideways from her lips, her hair was unkempt and the shoulder of her dress was pulled down in a revealing way. Two things kept me from laughing. Maria's face showed no sign of amusement. And she was a child, a little girl still in her teens.

When I offered to try to help Maria, she laughed.

'Me?' she said. 'There's no help for me.' And then she showed her needle-scarred arm, the badge of the mainliner.

My contact with Maria was short. We had not yet set up our programme for helping an addict. So all I could do was talk to her a few times, pray with her. To my surprise Maria claimed the prayers had set her free. She claimed a miracle. She *said* she was off heroin, but I always worried. Just those few prayers didn't seem enough.

Over the years I kept in touch with Maria but only sketchily. I heard that she was married and lived now on Coney Island. The thing I wanted most to know was whether or not she was clean: how successful had she been in staying off drugs?

Years passed. One day my Mother, who was working as my receptionist at the time, came bursting into my office at 416 Clinton Avenue.

'Guess who's here?'

'Jerry?' It was a plunge but I had been so worried

about my brother since the recent news that his marriage was breaking up because of alcohol.

'No, I'm afraid not. No, it's Maria.'

'Maria, you're kidding!' I jumped up and ran to the door and there stood Maria. She and Mother and I shook hands and laughed and exchanged greetings and then Maria and I had a talk.

'How're things now, Maria?' I asked.

'Well, I'm fine,' she said. It turned out that the reports about her had been accurate. She was indeed married, and did have children, and she was living on Coney Island. Most important, Maria told me that she was staying close to the Lord.

'And I'm off drugs, too. Really off them,' she said.

Maria wanted to see how our facilities were coming along. She had come by once when our induction centre consisted of four large rooms on the upper floor of the old mansion at 416 Clinton Avenue. In those days there had been no curtains on the windows, no rugs, no special effort to make the building attractive. Now the upstairs was more pleasant. The rooms were well decorated, bright, cheery.

And crowded. For at that particular moment we had a lot of boys in residence. We went from room to room, making introductions. 'This is the Maria from the book,' I said. Always the boys had to shake Maria's hand, and always their question was the same:

'Yeah? You still clean?'

When Maria said she had no more desire for dope, you could almost feel confidence pour into our boys.

Well, that's all I saw of Maria. She called Teen Challenge on a couple of other occasions, but always when I was not there. *I* might have thought it necessary to spend a lot of follow-up time with Maria, but I see now that according to the Holy Ghost's Timing we were not supposed to have a close and long relationship with this girl. His timing for her had been accomplished in one short, lightning encounter. That encounter changed everything. After that, we were no longer supposed to be in contact.

Israel was something else again.

Israel seems to have captured everyone's yearning. Because his story was incomplete people are always asking for news of him. They remember how, when I first preached to Israel's gang, the Mau Maus, Israel stuck out his hand like a gentleman. They remembered how he led the gang forward to accept the Lord during the rally at St. Nick's.

And they remembered how he fell, shortly after that. He was sentenced for five years to a reformatory on the charge of manslaughter in the first degree.

It wasn't until years later that I discovered that Israel's troubles were caused in part by a misunderstanding in which I played a role. And here again the principle of Holy Ghost Timing is very comforting. I don't want to suggest that the Holy Spirit *caused* this misunderstanding to take place, and created the suffering which followed. But I do suggest that when we goof, when we miss the Lord's timing due to our own weakness, or due to accident, or due to a failure in communication, Holy Ghost timing can redeem the mistake.

But about Israel. How well I remember the night he knelt on the platform of St. Nick's to commit his life to the Lord. I felt an unusual anointing of the Holy Spirit that night. If someone had suggested that Israel would soon go to prison on a murder charge, I'd have laughed.

What I didn't know was that at some point after his conversion Israel met with a disappointment. Then he made the biggest mistake of his life. He returned to the Mau Maus. A few months later he went to a rumble against a rival gang which resulted in the cold-blooded murder of a young man. Israel was charged with manslaughter in the first degree and sentenced for five years to a reformatory.

That was all of the story we knew. For some reason Israel was extraordinarily bitter. When we tried to reach him through his mother he would have nothing to do with us. So in time, we stopped trying.

It is here that Nicky Cruz enters the picture. Nicky and Israel accepted the Lord on the same night. If I had been asked to pick which of the two boys would become a giant for the Lord, I would certainly have picked Israel. Nicky Cruz was rather unprepossessing, stuttering, reserved. Israel was good-looking, with real presence and a dynamic quality that made people stop and take notice. I was looking on the outside, but God was looking at the heart. For it was Nicky who was to go on, and Israel who was incarcerated.

As I say, I eventually stopped trying to get in touch with Israel. Not so Nicky, bless him. One day the phone rang and a voice announced:

'Dave, this is Nicky Cruz.'

'Nicky!'

'Dave, I've got a surprise for you. I've just come from a prayer meeting. Guess who else was there. . .'

'I give up.'

'Israel.'

'You're kidding! How is he? Is he still bitter?'

'Not any more, Dave. For two reasons. First, this afternoon he gave his life to the Lord all over again. And second, we found out what happened to him that day he didn't show up — remember?'

How well I remembered. A few weeks after the crusade in St. Nicholas Arena, I was scheduled to hold another rally in Elmira, New York. I asked Nicky and Israel if they would like to go there with me. They went and gave their testimonies. Upon returning to New York City, I asked them if they'd like to accompany me to Philipsburg, Pennsylvania. We made arrangements to meet at 7:00 a.m. at the corner of Myrtle and DeKalb. I picked up Nicky. A mutual friend, who was to go with us, was scheduled to pick up Israel. We all waited from 7:00 a.m. until 9:30 a.m. No Israel. We called his house. No answer. We even *went* to his place; no one was at home. Discouraged, Nicky, our friend and I drove to Philipsburg by ourselves.

'Well, at least we now know what happened,' Nicky said on the phone. 'Israel was there all right, only he was waiting at another corner. Somebody got the place wrong. He had his bags packed a whole day ahead of time. He was so excited he was on his corner — Myrtle and Flatbush near the Manhattan Bridge in Brooklyn — at six in the morning. He waited and waited — until 11:00 a.m. Dave, this disappointment is the main reason Israel went back to the gang. He was that bitter.'

That explained a lot to me. I had always wondered.

And then Nick's voice dropped. 'Dave,' he said. 'You've got to call Israel. Right now. Will you?'

And, of course, I agreed. But I was very nervous. After

all, in a way I had been responsible for Israel's troubles. My hand was shaking so badly I had to get the secretary to dial the number. A voice answered: 'Hello.'

'Israel?'

'Yep.'

'Israel, do you remember St. Nicholas Arena when . . .'

'It's David!' Israel shouted into the phone. 'Hallelujah.'

And with that I knew everything was all right. Israel and I talked for a long time, mostly praising the Lord. Israel told me he was married now. Nicky had asked him to come to California to give his testimony, and he and his wife had accepted. They were leaving in a few minutes.

So I still didn't have a chance actually to see Israel. But the Lord took care of that, too. A few months later I was in Fresno, California on a crusade. Two hundred and fifty young people came to the counselling room. As I entered one fellow did a strange thing. He smiled and put his thumb to his forefinger in an okay sign. I nodded back, not knowing the man. A little later he came over and tapped me on the shoulder. His smile was broader than ever.

'Do I know you?' I asked.

'You should. I'm Israel. I've put on a little weight.'

'Israel!' We shook hands and he introduced me to his wife Rosa. Then and there I got Israel to give his testimony to the group of young people who had come counselling. He told it like it was, including the manslaughter charge.

'But praise the Lord, that's all past. I've learned one thing for sure,' Israel said. 'You can't run from the Lord.'

I've often puzzled over the Holy Ghost Timing in Israel's story. A mistaken street corner caused an awesome delay. At least that's the way it seems to me. Yet today Israel has a ministry of his own, and it's quite unique. He has a ministry to *losers*. On weekends he goes out giving his testimony and preaching. Today, when so many people have a ministry to winners — football heroes, baseball stars, Miss America beauties — Israel has a special word from the Lord for losers, the people who never quite make it. He has a patience, and a softness, and an understanding of the guy who doesn't end up a super-dude.

Would Israel have had such a dynamic ministry if we had met as planned? I don't know. All I do know is that the Lord redeemed our error. It took a while, but the main thing is that today Israel is in the Kingdom.

There, ahead of me, was Sonny Arguinzoni's church. It was just where I expected it to be: in a part of Los Angeles that was all Mexican-American. Not a ghetto mind — the Mexican-Americans are too proud to live in a ghetto — but this was a part of town that spoke of poverty and occasional violence.

The street in front of Sonny's church was crowded with cars. Sonny had spoken to me on the phone about his church. He said it was 'a little white clapboard building that will remind you of something from Pennsylvania'. And he was right. The building did take me back to my childhood in the mountains. I half-expected to find a pot-bellied stove and wooden benches inside.

Sonny had asked me to come to his church to take part in the installation of two new deacons. I was glad to do it. People sometimes accuse me of trying to turn all our young men into preachers. I suppose the criticism is fair, for to me full-time service to the Lord is the highest possible calling. So perhaps I was especially proud on this Sunday morning to be coming to the church of one of my own 'children'.

Sonny had started this church as a special service to ex-addicts like himself. Too many established churches, he told me, turn their backs on the addict. 'Once an addict always an addict,' they say. So Sonny started what he laughingly calls the All Junkie Church in East Los Angeles.

Of course, the church isn't made up entirely of junkies. In fact Sonny's ministry stresses the *families* of junkies, for Sonny knows from experience that they face special problems. Wives have to get used to the fact that they are no longer living with devils incarnate. Children have to get used to the fact that they have parents again.

In front of me on the street now was the little knot of men who had spotted my car and who were directing me with grand flourishes to a reserved parking place. These were Sonny's deacons, neatly dressed men, each in a good, well-cut Sunday best. And standing slightly in the background were their wives; they too were smartly dressed; almost all were holding the hands of small children, each done out in bright fresh colours. With great dignity the deacons walked me inside the church where Sonny was waiting.

How could this possibly be the same Sonny Arguinzoni I had known just a few years ago! He seemed physically taller than before. Certainly he was carrying a little something extra around the middle; coming off drugs so often seems to have this effect. Sonny greeted me with warmth. The only thing missing was the usual Pentecostal bearhug; somehow the moment was too formal. Sonny gave a short speech about how glad they all were to have me come, then without further talk we moved down the aisle. I took my place on the platform and watched as, below me, about thirty young children sat down in the front rows. The church was packed out. And as Sonny gathered the group together in song, I relived the experiences in Holy Ghost timing that led up to this moment.

I met Sonny not long after I found Shorty and his friends on the rooftop of my Second Avenue Trysting Place, swishing hypodermic needles in a Coca-Cola bottle full of dirty water, and determined that I would not preach again until I was certain I had something to say.

I found young Sonny leaning against a lamp post beneath an elevated train in the Bedford-Stuyvesant district of Brooklyn. I remember that there was a pizza store near by. The poor kid — he must have weighed everything of 120 pounds. His eyes were sunken, dark, as if someone had hit him. He stood lolling up against the post, so drowsy that he seemed to be dropping to sleep as I tried to talk to him.

At first Sonny would have nothing to do with me. He thought I was a narcotics agent. When I suggested a pizza however — I remember I said I'd buy him a pepperoni — he brightened just a little. We ate with me doing a monologue and with Sonny dozing. I said I'd come back another day, and if I found him around I'd try anchovies with him this time.

Well, over pizzas Sonny and I gradually came to know each other, though it was clear Sonny still wondered what I was up to. Then one day I let it out that I was going to be holding a service in a small Puerto Rican church in the neighbourhood. None of Sonny's junkie friends wanted to miss that — a Narco trying to pull off a sermon. There were two things wrong with that: I wasn't a narcotics agent, and I wasn't going to preach, I was going to put myself out on a limb with a promise. Come to Jesus and His Spirit will free you of your addiction.

The day for the service came. Gang members sporting incongruous alpine hats and carrying canes, junkies strung out on heroin, their girls, all sorts and conditions of kids flocked into the little church that night to see the show. At the end of the praise service I gave an altar call. A small group of junkies came forward, including Sonny. I told him that I felt God had His hand on him and I asked him if he would come stay with Gwen and me until God had done His work.

Sonny came along in a half stupor. I'll never forget my introduction to 'cold turkey' withdrawal. That night I watched as Sonny's legs jerked violently and perspiration soaked his pyjamas. One moment he shivered from cold, and the next he threw back his covers trying to shake off hot flushes. Goose-bumps which made him look like a dressed fowl were visible over his arms and neck.

I needed to go to Brooklyn on one of the following days and I didn't want to leave Sonny alone so I asked him if he'd come along. As soon as we crossed the bridge I noticed the boy's restlessness return. Suddenly he was crying, 'Let me out! It's no use. I've got to have a fix.' I tried to argue with him but he opened the car door when I came to a light and leaped from the car.

So Sonny went back on drugs!

I remember talking to Gwen about whether I should quit and go back to Philipsburg. 'I don't see what I can do here,' I said. 'I failed with Sonny.'

'Now, Dave,' said Gwen. 'In the first place I'm sure you're never going to have one hundred per cent success;

you've got to work with *more* boys before you can make a decision. And beyond that,' she smiled, 'how do you know what Christ may have in mind for Sonny?'

Gwen was right. The Lord did have something special in mind for Sonny, but He had to wait for the boy to get desperate first. That took several months. But then Sonny got himself into trouble. He was getting further addicted. He ran out of money, started to steal, and once was shot in the leg. More months passed during which I lost track of the boy while he was sinking further into his private hell.

In the meanwhile we had launched our work at Teen Challenge, and had a few successes. Among them was a boy named Chino who had once been a friend of Sonny Arguinzoni. Later we learned about the day Chino ran into Sonny, lolling as usual around a street corner.

'Hey, Man,' said Sonny, 'good to see you out.'

Sonny assumed that Chino had been in prison because he no longer had the tight look of a man strung out on heroin. But Chino had another story. He told Sonny how Christ had pulled him out of the pit and saved him. Of course Sonny didn't believe him. Chino invited Sonny to go with him to the Teen Challenge Centre in Brooklyn. Sonny accepted with the thought that the centre must be some sort of of dance club.

Sonny ended up by fully committing his life to Christ and the next day he realised that this centre had been founded by the same 'skinny country preacher' who once had taken him into his home. In Sonny's case the Holy Spirit waited for that Moment of Desperation, before He reached inside the boy's soul and transformed it.

But transform it He did.

For here, now, standing before me on the platform of

this little clapboard church in East Los Angeles, was this same Sonny. I just sat there revelling in the miracle. I could see it not only in Sonny but in the scores of families who were also finding the sustaining, carrying power of the Holy Spirit at work in their lives.

That day we did install two new deacons. Sonny and I stood side by side and placed our hands on their heads. The Holy Spirit anointed us all in a special way. I said, at the edge of tears, 'Thank You Lord for the high privilege of being here with Sonny Arguinzoni and his extended family in the Lord. Thank You. Thank You.'

So what I was learning was simple: I was to do my best in the Lord's work, do what seems right at the time and trust Him with the rest.

At first I thought Holy Ghost timing had to do mostly with a sudden, dramatic about-face in a person's life. But His timing is equally crisp and important in other parts of spiritual growth as well.

For instance, I have discovered that just as a child must break away from his parents in order to mature, so a spiritual child must leave home too.

And it is not always easy.

With my good friend Nicky Cruz, for example, I gave too much fatherly advice when fatherly advice was no longer called for. Naturally I thought it was good advice.

'Don't ever be a "carbon copy" of me,' I said, as if he ever considered it. 'Instead,' I said, 'be a "carbon copy" of Jesus.'

'Remember what my grandfather used to say, Nicky,' I said, '"God always makes way for a praying man."'

'Never let your past hold you down,' I said.

And I also said, 'Never be under bondage to any man.'

Nicky took these advices seriously, especially the part about never being under bondage to any man. He started his own independent ministry quite early, and just as any father might do, I constantly hovered in the background, worrying about him.

'What if Nicky fails,' I asked the Lord late at night. And the Lord corrected me gently: 'If I have been able to keep *you*, I certainly can keep Nicky.'

And all the time, of course, Nicky was doing fabulously well. Ever since he knelt at St. Nicholas Arena, Nicky had been advancing spiritually. His ministry, his books, his movie were all giant killers. Billy Graham was calling him 'a legend in our time'. Nicky was growing rapidly, but — more important it seemed to me — he was growing steadily. No, Holy Ghost timing in this case did not have to do with Nicky, it had to do with me. It was really time for me to let this fabulous young man go, to realise that it was really inappropriate for me to keep on giving him 'advice'.

There was a definite, specific night when I relinquished Nicky. I remember it very well. It was about three o'clock in the morning, and I was getting tired and ready for bed. 'Lord Jesus, You converted Nicky, You are keeping him. I turn him over to You and to Your keeping.'

'Good.' The Lord seemed almost to have shouted at me.

And, as almost always happens in natural relationships, this relinquishment was the making of a new and far healthier tie with Nicky.

I knew it one day when I got an invitation from him to hold a joint crusade on his turf, as it were. Nicky invited me to California.

I found that I was delighted. I accepted.

What I didn't know was that Nicky had something

cooked up for me. A little surprise. We preached for forty-five minutes, shot-gun style. This was a term Nicky and I had developed for a rather unusual form of a joint crusade preaching. Nicky would talk for five minutes, then I would talk for five minutes, then Nicky would talk for five. It was astonishing how Nicky could pick up on my thoughts and I on his, we were that closely attuned that evening. We hardly missed a beat. The kids took it as a sort of game and really enjoyed it. And still there was power. The Spirit Himself was there, anointing.

But when it was all over Nicky stood at the microphone and said:

'Now, folks, we have a very special gift for Dave tonight. As you know, he is my spiritual father. I really love this man and I have tried to follow in his footsteps. And now, with your permission, I would like to show you a little bit of the results.'

With that, Nicky left the pulpit and went offstage. Within a minute he came back on to the platform like a pied piper, trailing behind him a herd of little boys, diddy-boppers, all about twelve years old. They were scrubbed and shining. But there was a quality of light coming from them that did not belong to the washcloth. There was absolutely no mistaking it. The light of Christ was in their eyes.

Nicky grouped the boys around him in a semi-circle at the front of the stage. I counted eleven boys. Then, when he had them all lined up he drew me into the circle too and said the words which drew applause from the crowd and tears from my own eyes.

'Boys,' Nicky said. 'Boys, I want you to meet your grandfather.'

When the whistles and the clapping died down, one of

the little boys stepped forward and said quite simply, looking at me, 'Mister, I'm sure glad you got Nicky because Nicky got me.'

I would liked to have added that I was sure glad Jesus had got us all. But there was this lump in my throat that wouldn't let me.

3

Two Profitless Success Stories

Each of us needs to learn – even if the lesson is painful – that our work doesn't belong to us.

FOR NEITHER THE publisher in the United States nor for the producer of the film has *The Cross and the Switchblade* been a financial success.

This, in spite of the fact, that recently I saw an advertisement stating that the bookhas sold 11,000,000 copies. This figure may, or may not, be accurate. I know that — as will become plain — I have not started dressing Gwen in mink because of the royalty income. In some cases we have just not received our royalties. For instance, on that trip to Europe which we just finished, we visited many of the publishers who are printing the book in foreign language editions. There are 24 translations now. It was difficult for us even to find out how many copies had been sold.

And as to the movie, it got kind reviews from such surprising sources as the *New York Times*. Critics found the movie well done, in which opinion grass roots America must have agreed, for the movie as of this writing has grossed more than $6,000,000 and still has its television life ahead of it. Yet, for the producer it was financially a failure.

All of which goes to prove in an odd way that *The*

Cross and the Switchblade was God's project from the very beginning and still remains so. Only God was supposed to get the glory from the work. I know that this was the prayer which surrounded the book. John and Elizabeth Sherrill, who co-authored *The Cross and the Switchblade* with me, quite literally prayed over each page of the manuscript as it was being written; and later without knowing that they had been proceeding in this way, I did the same. The prayer was that the glory go to the Lord. He honoured that prayer with a little extra fillip by seeing to it that the glorious mind-boggling pot of gold at the end of the rainbow turned into a fantasy. For with every dollar we did receive in royalties from the movie and the book, many more have vanished.

John and Tib Sherrill and I have been a little surprised at our reaction to all this. Except for a short period of time, when we were caught off guard, we early came to see the whole failure story almost with a sense of humour. Not that we exactly had a belly laugh. It was more the quiet chuckle, the kind that can only come when you know you are really being taken care of; the kind that comes with a security so immense that it shrugs off as a minor detail such events as having your ship come on, only to sink in the harbour.

All of which takes a bit of explaining. How did *The Cross and the Switchblade* come to be written?

At a certain point of the unfolding story of Teen Challenge a strange thing began to happen to me. During my late-night meetings with the Lord, my mind became more focused on the story of the Samaritans when they were surrounded by the armies of Ben-hadad, King of Syria. As a result of the siege there was a great famine in Samaria. Four lepers sat outside the city gates and they too were starving. The lepers decided that they might as well surrender since they were going to die anyhow. They journeyed out to the army encampment and discovered that it was empty! A sudden devastation had struck the Syrians and they had fled. The lepers looked in astonishment at the booty which lay in the fields just waiting to be enjoyed. They rushed back to Samaria to tell the famine-stricken city of all the loot available in the vacant camp (II Kings 7:3-9).

This is exactly the way I felt. Here I was sitting with immense wealth at my fingertips, the wealth of the Lord. It was a fortune that was just waiting to be picked up. But first I had to tell people about it. How? How? How could I shout the news loud enough?

At this point in time Gwen and I had a visit from a friend, Harald Bredesen. Harald has a rather unique gift from the Holy Spirit. He is a catalyst. He puts people together and things happen.

Harald was at our house. Gwen and I were talking with him about our feeling that we wanted to share the great wealth of the Lord. Never one to be shy about such things, Harald bowed his head then and there and began to pray.

'Lord Jesus,' he said, with an exuberance that belongs almost uniquely to him, 'help us. Praise Your name, Jesus. Amen.' And then without any transition, he went on. 'I know a couple of writers. John and Tib Sherrill over at *Guideposts*. Do you want to see if I can make a date?'

And the next thing I knew we were sitting with the Sherrills working on a story for the magazine. It was the first time *Guideposts* magazine had ever run a multiple-part article. There were three instalments in all. I didn't learn until later how difficult it was for John and Tib to get the story past the doubting eye of some of the most respected members of the magazine's editorial board. By its non-profit charter *Guideposts* is an inter-faith publication encouraging people of all faiths to draw from their own religious heritage. Even the Christians on the staff come from a wide variety of persuasions. Those members of the board who had not yet been in contact with Pentecost were sceptical of the stories of miracle and power which the Sherrills submitted.

'At least let's check it out,' one of the staffers said. And they did. In good journalistic tradition, without consulting me first, *Guideposts* telephoned around the country to talk with people mentioned in my story; they went to the newspapers covering the Michael Farmer murder trial; they came down to Teen Challenge. The story checked out to their satisfaction: editor Len LeSourd then made his final decision to publish.

The impact of those articles was astonishing. It was clear to me, as it was to *Guideposts*, that the general American public was very anxious indeed to hear the Good News that the God of Abraham, Isaac and Jacob still lives. John and Tib and I soon found ourselves talking about a book. There was only one problem; the Sherrills estimated that to do the job correctly would require about three years. How ever would any of us find the time necessary for this kind of deep, intensive research and writing?

So we decided to put out a fleece.

This was the first time John and Tib had ever heard of a fleece, and they were sceptical. We read over together the account in Judges where Gideon 'put out a fleece' at a point where he had to make a major decision in an effort to reassure himself that he was in the will of the Lord. Gideon placed a lamb's fleece on the ground one dewy night and asked the Lord to let the fleece be dry but to let the ground around the fleece be wet the next morning: this would be a sign that he was in the Lord's will. The prayer was answered and, after a confirmation, Gideon moved forward.

Now I have a feeling that fleeces should be used sparingly. They should be placed before the Lord, I think, only when we are looking for a *divine mandate* on a really important decision. When we have tried all other guidance systems and are still not sure what to do, then is the time to place the strongest possible question before the Lord, seeking His assurance. Except for times such as this our faith should be in the Word, not in the wool. Otherwise, instead of seeking the Lord, we spend our time running around checking the dew.

In our case, since such huge chunks of time were involved for everyone, this certainly did seem an appropriate moment for a fleece. John and Tib and I talked about this late one Friday afternoon. We decided to put out the fleece and to make it a difficult one. First, Bernard Geis, the publisher John had in mind, should grant us an immediate appointment even though it was already four o'clock, just before the weekend. Second, Mr. Geis should agree to invest what was to us a large sum of money, $5,000, to insure his interest in the project and to cover the high editorial cost involved in the three years we would need to produce the manuscript. And thirdly, that we leave the publisher's office with a basic agreement about the contract.

Okay, why not. We all shook hands, prayed about it and then picked up the phone. We found Geis in. He explained that he was leaving for the weekend in an hour, but if we came right over he could see us. So at 4:30 John and Tib and I were sitting in Geis' book-lined office. The man was a bit preoccupied with signing cheques but he asked John to explain his project. So John plunged into a statistical recap of the results we were getting with drug addicted kids. Geis didn't seem interested. Ten minutes passed. Finally John said,

'Excuse me, Mr. Geis, I think I'm going in the wrong direction. Let me just tell you the story of this skinny country preacher.' And so for 20 minutes John launched into the *story* of what had happened to me since my first encounters with the Lord on Albert Hill. Bernard Geis put down his pen, leaned back in his chair and listened. At five o'clock he looked at his watch.

'Well, I've heard enough. You've got a deal. We'll work out the details later. Will you be wanting an advance?'

'Yes. Five thousand dollars.'

Bernard Geis stood up and held out both hands to us. 'We're on,' he said. 'I'll send you the papers. Excuse me, I must leave now.'

So the fleece was answered. We had our mandate.

That very next Monday we began work. John said a simple prayer. 'God,' he said, 'help us to tell this story honestly. Help us to tell it Your way. Amen.' Then I found myself staring down the muzzle of a tape-recorder microphone.

John and Tib and I certainly had no thought of an international best-seller as we began our work. We spent fourteen months on the research aspects of the story. There were the Monday sessions after work at John's office. There were sessions at the Sherrills' house. There were meetings with the young people at Teen Challenge. And all the while the Sherrills were working on the early drafts. I was anxious to know how the manuscript was reading, but John and Tib were careful not to let me see the early work. All in all there were six different rewrites of the entire book.

I did not know until later about a prayer aspect of the project. John and Tib were praying over each individual page in a rather unique way. At the top of the page they would write out a series of letters, varying from page to page. It might go something like this: LBWUAWWOTP, which would stand for LORD BE WITH US AS WE WORK ON THIS PAGE or, LTIATPHUSIP, which would stand for LORD THIS IS A TOUGH PROBLEM. HELP US SOLVE IT, PLEASE.

Finally the day came when they called to tell me that the manuscript was in the mail. When it arrived I took it into the prayer-room Gwen and I had built in the garage back of our house. I sat down in the overstuffed chair where I do much of my praying, took the manuscript into my lap and started to read. As familiar as I was with the story, on many occasions it brought tears to my own eyes. When I was through, I got down on my knees and without knowing how the Sherrills had prayed over each page, I found myself doing exactly the same thing. I literally took each separate page and prayed over it. I had two criteria. 'Lord is this the truth as I remember it?' and, 'Lord, does this glorify You?' Any place where both of these criteria were not met, I marked the manuscript for correction. We wanted to be immaculately careful.

There was only one portion of the manuscript which bothered me seriously. And I tell this as a point of confession because it shows how I can be seduced by the good opinion of *men,* instead of letting the Lord work in His own way.

I had trouble with the last chapter. In it John and Tib had written about the Pentecostal side of our work. Suddenly there it was, ready to go into print that we spoke in tongues at 416 Clinton Avenue. I had spent years trying to get the social agencies in New York to accept us as a proper house of therapy, years trying to get the courts and the jails to co-operate with us. And now I was afraid we would become the laughing stock of these same institutions. The charismatic renewal had not yet become acceptable; we were still living in a day when Pentecostals were considered Holy Ghost bumpkins. If we told it like it was, I worried — if we talked about how our young people raised their hands and praised the Lord and spoke in languages which were not their own — would this hurt us?

It was Bernard Geis who settled the issue. We decided to put the question of the last chapter aside for a moment and see how Mr. Geis responded to the rest of the book.

And then a very peculiar thing happened.

I got a call from John and Tib, each speaking on an extension in their home. 'We've heard from Geis,' John said. 'He liked the manuscript, Davie, except for one thing. He asked whether or not we believe in this business about speaking in tongues.'

'What does he mean? It's in the book.'

'I know,' Tib said. 'But he said we were writing as if we were afraid of the subject. He wants us to take that last chapter back, turn it into two chapters. He wants us to get *into* the Baptism of the Holy Spirit and write about it the way we feel.'

So the end of the book was rewritten once more. This time we put ourselves on the line, we talked pointedly about the source of the power we were working with. When I knelt one final time to pray over each page of these last two chapters, chills raced through me, for I knew that there was no turning back.

And I knew something else too. I saw now why the Lord had chosen Bernard Geis, who is Jewish, to publish this Christ-centred book. The reason was very simple. If we had taken the story to almost any Christian publisher in those days, their reaction to that last chapter would have been the opposite of Bernard Geis'. 'Tongues are too controversial,' they would have said. 'You'd better tone that down.' And because of my own timidity at the time I probably would have followed this advice. Bernard Geis on the other hand singled out 'speaking in tongues' as the element he wanted to highlight. Geis' motive, doubtless, was good journalism. The Lord's motive was something else again.

Later, two incidents occurred which were to confirm why the Lord had chosen Geis. A top Christian publisher came to us with an offer for a huge printing of the book in Spanish. 'There is a problem though,' the publisher said. 'You would have to take out those last two chapters.' We turned the offer down. The Spanish version which finally did appear, from another house, has sold better than any foreign language edition.

The only foreign edition which did not succeed was a European one in which, unknown to us, the last two chapters were simply deleted. When we found this out we insisted on another edition which would include the last two chapters. And (I don't know why we should be surprised!) this time the book took off and did extremely well.

We were staggered at the impact of *The Cross and the Switchblade*. With very little advertising, the book's sales curve began to rise. Year after year, it has been one of the nation's best sellers. It wasn't long before we began to get serious inquiries from Hollywood. Even though Bernard Geis controlled the movie rights, most of the inquiries were made directly to me. We had seven offers from Hollywood producers and major scriptwriters. When these came in I got on the line for another conference call with Tib and John.

'Davie,' John said, 'our business is books, not movies. You make the decision. We won't muddy the waters. The only thing that I do suggest is that you watch your safeguards.'

'Safeguards?' Tib commented. 'Chances are you won't get script approval, so you'd better just be sure of your producer and your star.'

That made sense to me. So in my prayer time I asked, 'Lord, if You want this movie to be done, please find a solid Christian to play the lead. And also a Christian producer who understands the message.'

When I told Bernard Geis I was turning down offers, his main concern was that I be clear in my thinking.

'Just what *do* you want?' Geis asked. 'Maybe we can help.'

'Well, I'll be frank, Mr. Geis. I want a Christian to produce the show and I want a Christian to act my part.'

Geis was silent for a long time. You could almost hear the shrug of his shoulders through his voice. 'Well, you're turning down some very good offers. They can make you a great deal of money.' With all the difficulties we eventually had with Bernard Geis' bankruptcy, I shall always appreciate the way he left this matter of the movie strictly in my hands.

One offer did come closer than the rest. I got a telephone call from Bernard Geis one day, his voice excited.

'David,' Geis said. 'I think we're on our way. Pat Boone's a Christian, isn't he?'

How would Pat himself have answered that question I wondered.

My silence didn't encourage Geis very much. I could hear that shrug in his voice again.

'Well, he's trying to buy the rights, anyway. What do you want me to do?'

'I'd like to talk with him. Do you think you could set it up?'

A few weeks later Gwen and I were sitting with Pat in an Italian restaurant in mid-town New York. Pat was in town to do a summer fill-in series on television. He sure was Hollywood! Tanned, dramatic hair, bright white shoes, western clothes. But both Gwen and I found a sincerity and warmth in him which we responded to right away. Pat told us that he had picked up a copy of *The Cross and the Switchblade* at an airport news-stand in Mexico City. 'You know what it's like on location,' he said. 'You have to be up at dawn. Well, I got to reading that book late one night, and simply couldn't put it down. I'd like to produce the movie. And I would like you to play your own part.'

I had a quick answer for that one. I was not going to get into acting. I was too busy working on the streets, and that's what I told Pat.

'The first question is to find the right producer,' I said, thinking of my prayer. And then I broached the question. 'I wonder if you'd be willing to talk with the members of our Teen Challenge Board?'

What Pat didn't know was that I had set up this meeting rather carefully. I had asked half a dozen busy men to give up an evening to help me make a decision I simply was not willing to make by myself. It had to do with Pat's 'spiritual maturity'. I shudder now at my presumption. The difficulty, of course, is that any time you set yourself up to check on another man's 'spiritual maturity' you're in danger of judgmentalism and pride. I thought that by getting others to help me I would avoid the trap. It didn't work out that way.

The meeting was to take place at Glad Tidings Tabernacle, located on a dark side street just south of Times Square, where muggings and robberies are commonplace. I was familiar with the church and I knew how fabulously God had used this congregation both in New York and on the mission field. But Pat, doubtless, was more aware of the drunken woman who stumbled towards us just as we reached Glad Tidings.

Even as we made our way down the dim echoing steps, I began to have doubts about what we were doing. Inside the basement auditorium sat half a dozen men from the Board of Teen Challenge. Suddenly they seemed to me to be a grilling team. Pat and Gwen and I sat in folding chairs with our backs to the cold wall. In an effort to retrieve the monstrous situation I found myself trying to sell Pat. I talked about his clean living and the jokes in Hollywood about his milk drinking and about his good family life. The Board tried to ask the two questions they really cared about. Was Pat saved? Did he know the Holy

Ghost? Somehow no one put the questions outright. Every time we tried we just sank farther into our own quagmire.

At the end of ten minutes I could see that we had gone far enough.

'Pat, this is ridiculous,' I said. 'But I must tell you why we've got you here. I asked the Lord for a sign. I've asked that if He wants me to do this movie He find a sold-out Christian for the producer and for the lead.'

Pat stood. His smile was so contagious. It put us all at ease, and got us off our own hook. Pat raised his hands waist high, palms up. 'Well, gentlemen. All I can say is that I am trying.'

After he left, Gwen and the Board and I had quite a prayer meeting. The gist of it was very simple. 'Lord, so much about Pat seems right. We pray for him to have a real encounter with You and with Your Spirit.'

Three years passed. They were years in which other people made lucrative offers for the movie, but they missed so badly filling the criteria of my prayer that there was no problem in turning them down.

Then one day I had a telephone call from a producer named Dick Ross. I knew a little about him already. He had worked on Billy Graham films, so I took it for granted that I was talking with a Christian. Ross asked if he could come see me when he was in New York the following week. Gwen and Dick and I did meet, and Dick outlined to us the approach he had in mind for the film. I liked it from the beginning.

'I'll tell you what I want to do,' Dick said. 'I want to tell the story as it is, and yet I want it to be a family movie without unnecessary blood and gore, and without tawdry sex.'

'Well, that part sounds good,' I said.

'Who do you have in mind for the lead?' Gwen asked.

'A friend of yours, Pat Boone.'

I stared straight ahead. But then Dick said something that made me realise he already knew about the previous contact with Boone.

'Pat asked me to pass a message on to you. He said, "Tell Gwen and David that I have experienced the last two chapters of their book."'

I looked at Gwen and laughed. 'If Pat has received the Holy Spirit,' I said, 'then he is the man. It looks like the prayer has been answered. I'll talk with the Sherrills and we'll see about getting the rights for you.'

So Dick Ross did buy the rights to *The Cross ana the Switchblade*. They were possibly sold for a record low in Hollywood: $10,000 divided five ways between Bernard Geis, the agent Evelyn Singer, myself and the Sherrills.

On the day the papers were to be signed, Gwen and I and our staff began a new prayer campaign. This time it had to do with the Spirit's guiding of the film. Our prayer was fivefold. First, that the film be an evangelical tool. Second, that everybody taking part in the movie be touched and changed by the story. Third, that in the translation from printed page to celluloid, the essential story remain intact. Fourth, that gore and sex not be exploited in the making of the picture. And fifth, that the producer stay away from any faked-up Pentecostal experiences just for the sake of sensationalism.

The Lord gave us an early sign that He was really in this film by adding a dividend. The person chosen to direct the movie was Don Murray, a fine Christian. Don called us one day with news that the script was finished. Could we talk it over with him? So it was that Gwen and I invited Don Murray to dinner.

In order to understand what happened next I need to touch on another development that has taken place in our family since *The Cross and the Switchblade*. In the first part of that story I tell of selling our television set in order not to be tempted to watch late-night shows when I should be praying. People have often asked if we ever went back to watching television and the answer is yes. After several years we received freedom in the Lord to enjoy TV in our home when it seemed appropriate.

One of the shows that our six-year-old son Greggy watched was 'The Outcasts' starring Don Murray as a cowboy. On the night that Don came to our house for dinner, we couldn't figure out why Greggy wasn't at his place. I was just about to go look for him when the door flew open and in dashed Greg, pistols drawn and fully dressed as a western gunfighter. I started to laugh, but then I got a look at Don's face. He did not laugh at all, but spoke to Greg straight.

'Greg, if I had known you were one of my fans,' Don said, 'I would have worn *my* cowboy outfit.'

Greggy fairly glowed. All through dinner he sat with his hands on his gun, ready to draw. Fortunately for us, the occasion never arose.

I suggested to Don that we take advantage of a good piece of luck. Nicky Cruz was in town. 'Why don't we go to his hotel, and we'll all read the script together.'

Don was delighted. So we drove into Manhattan and at about ten o'clock that night Nicky and I began to read the manuscript.

I started with page one and read with a sinking heart. I didn't recognise myself. Still, I did not want to say a thing to influence Nicky. Finally he put the script down.

'Well?'

'I've only got one thing to say, Davie. This'll kill you.'

Don looked at me.

'Nicky, you said it for me,' I said. 'I'm sorry, Don.'

'Don't be sorry,' Don said. 'We've paid for the script. It is ours. We can do with it what we want.' He rolled up his sleeves. 'Let's get to work.'

Checking with us constantly, Don rewrote the manuscript then and there. Nicky and I stayed up with him all night and through most of the next day with only a few moments out for rest. 'There's just one place where I'd like to take a stand, Don,' I said towards the end of the marathon. 'You are winding the story up at St. Nicholas Arena. Will you let *me* rewrite the sermon?'

It must have been a difficult decision for Don, but he agreed. It was strange how the Lord quickened my memory. I could even recall specific phrases. I remembered how, as I talked about the power of love, those hostile boys and girls grew quiet. I could recall the way the Spirit began to move on them, bringing tears. I could recall the shuffling feet, the restlessness.

Just as it had been the Holy Spirit who originally preached that sermon, so now the Holy Spirit recreated His message. When I gave it to Don, and he read it through it seemed to me that his relief was visible.

'David, you've done it. We won't change a word.'

So our prayers were being answered one by one. The

gospel message was intact, and in a key spot in the story — right at the end. I was satisfied that the film had not exploited blood, sex, and gore. The treatment left the story essentially intact, even though, of course, it could not be as complete as the book. All in all I had a good feeling about the project.

One amusing change was added to the script several days later. The character of Little JoJo underwent a mutation and became a girl.

The Little JoJo of the book, it seemed, was destined from the beginning to be a person people wanted to mutate. In actual life JoJo was a teenage boy. But after the book appeared, a group of nondescript men from all over the country began claiming that they were the Little JoJo of David Wilkerson's book. I've seen posters showing grizzly old men holding up copies of the Bible and *The Cross and the Switchblade*. The poster caption said, 'Tonight. Come hear Little JoJo. Straight out of the pages of *The Cross and the Switchblade.*' Other men, also claiming this identification were wandering from town to town raising money for orphanages in Mexico and Guatemala.

So Little JoJo had already mysteriously aged about forty years. Now, he changed sex. It happened in this way.

As Don Murray and Dick Ross began try-outs for various parts in the movie, a young, black actor appeared to read for the part of JoJo. It was a bright reading. Don and Dick and Pat were all delighted. But when the try-out was over JoJo pulled off his cap and down fell mounds of hair. The reader was a girl!

'Would you mind,' Don asked, over the long-distance line, 'if the part were played by a girl? She's brilliant.'

'What about the sermon?'

'It's untouched.'

'Then I say let's go ahead.'

To this day it is beyond me how anyone can make a movie out of the confusion that takes place on location.

Don Murray and his troupe moved into New York with all the hurry-scurry, all the technical talk, all the complicated equipment of Hollywood. How these people could ever take a portion of this, a shot of that, a retake of the other, put it all together and come up with a continuous story, was thoroughly beyond my understanding.

The person I most wanted to talk to again was Pat Boone. Gwen and I had not seen him since his encounter with the Holy Spirit. Now we met at the church of the Reverend Vincente Ortiz, in whose home I had lived when I first came to New York. St. Nicholas Arena had been torn down since the writing of the book, so we were using the auditorium of the church of Reverend Ortiz.

Reverend Ortiz is the man who first opened my eyes to what it was like to be a dedicated Christian in a ghetto. I remember asking him why he wanted to live here when his wife was afraid to walk to the corner for a quart of milk, and his teenage daughter was afraid of rape in the hallways at school.

'Why do we stay?' Vincente said. 'Because God has called us here.' That was all he ever said — or needed to say — on the subject.

Vincente Ortiz was among the first to help me realise

the heroism of many ghetto Christians. These men and women created a haven of the Spirit amid violence and frustration. Their lives centred around the Church. At first I was confused at the way his congregation sang so loudly and even danced in the aisles of the church. But then it dawned on me that this was all *praise*, and that praise was their chief weapon against the evils of the ghetto. In a short while I became convinced that the Lord was well pleased indeed with this church.

Pat Boone was standing outside Reverend Ortiz's church when I saw him. He was made up for my part, and I had to chuckle.

Pat had once heard our friend and supporter, Walter Hoving, the president of Tiffany's, say, 'I like David Wilkerson because he looks like he's just come off a mountaintop fast: lean and gaunt.?' Pat certainly looked as if he'd been on a fast. But make-up wasn't enough for him. I found him watching my every gesture, evidently trying to copy my mannerisms for authenticity in the movie. It made me nervous.

Pat went with me for two days to meet my gutter world. I took him to all my favourite street corners and began to introduce him to junkies. Of course, Pat had on his famous white buck shoes, and he looked pretty Hollywood. We stopped right in the heart of 'Little Korea' in the Bronx. Word soon spread — 'Hey, the cat himself is here. Pat Boone.' They mobbed us, and to my surprise Pat used the occasion to preach Christ. While he was talking, I could hear the guys saying, 'Hey, heavy man. That's all right.' And of course everybody — upon finding out that Pat was making a movie — started following him around trying to get a part. Kids rolled up their sleeves saying, 'Hey, look. I'm a bigger junkie than anybody on the block.'

On the second day I took Pat to the rooftops, into dark basement rooms where kids stuck dirty needles into their veins. A few minutes later Pat said he could never be the same again. 'For me, this is going to be more than a movie, David. I see it as the greatest spiritual challenge of my life.'

Something about his sincerity made me want to be utterly honest with him. I had to tell him about the first time I heard he might play the part. I remember that I turned to Gwen and said, 'What is Pat going to do? Walk through Harlem singing April Love to those junkies? We'd better start praying.'

Pat laughed and admitted that he'd been having the same doubts about himself. 'Just keep up the prayers, won't you?' he said.

We were back at Vincente Ortiz' church. Pat left us to make up, for in a short while the shooting would start on the all-important scene, the sermon. Gwen and I went inside and took seats near the back of the church. Soon we were joined by Pat's wife, Shirley who had flown in from Hollywood especially to be here for this one session.

Shirley looked as glamorous as Hollywood and was full of the Spirit as Pat.

'Know what we've been doing?' Shirley asked. 'Fasting. For three days. Both of us.' So Pat's gaunt look wasn't just make-up! 'Everything depends upon this one little eight-minute scene. It's the Holy Spirit's sermon. I wish you'd go back and talk with him, David,' Shirley said. 'Pray with him.'

So I did. Pat was standing aside ready to be called. I

was astonished to see tears in his eyes. 'David, will you lay hands on me?' Pat asked. It must have said a lot to the non-Christians in the crew, watching Pat look to prayer for help.

'I'd like you to ask for something special to happen,' Pat went on. 'Because of course I'm *not* David Wilkerson and this is not St. Nicholas Arena. And I'm not the best actor in the world. And still this scene has got to come across. Only the Lord can do that.'

So we prayed. I put my hands on Pat's shoulder and asked the Spirit to move through him. Then Pat went before the cameras, and I walked back to take my seat beside Shirley and Gwen.

We heard Don Murray call for quiet. 'Lights, camera. . . he said. 'Action!' And suddenly there Pat was, speaking the words which I had said so many years ago, almost exactly as they had originally been given me. This was the Holy Spirit's message. I began to shake with the Spirit's quaking. I knew that something extraordinary was taking place before the camera. Pat was not acting. The Holy Ghost was anointing him as a preacher. Shirley reached over and took hold of my arm. She squeezed; her fingers dug into my flesh.

'It's God,' she whispered. 'It's God. The Spirit is here.'

The scene had to be done in several takes. But the anointing on Pat was so strong that he was able to move from take to take without once losing the Spirit.

Once, while the technicians were doing whatever technicians do and there was a break, one of the young actors came up to me.

'David,' he said. 'Would you mind praying for me?'

I was surprised. But the boy went on. 'First I'd better tell you that when I started this part, it was just another role to me, something I was doing because I liked the job. I don't go to church, and I've never had an experience with Christ.

'But you know,' he went on, 'I'm feeling what these boys must have felt. I've got to get up there now and surrender my life to God. When I do, I don't want to be acting. I want it to be for real.'

It was all I could do to keep from praising the Lord at the top of my lungs. Certainly I would pray for him. When I finished the young actor was struggling against tears.

Then the shooting of his scene began again. Once more I was back in St. Nick's. I was reliving that moment as if it were happening all over again. And I knew as I watched that this was not just a group of actors reaching out for reality. It was a real 'happening'.

It was an astonishing experience. I knew at that moment that this was going to be a special film, indeed.

Gwen touched my arm. I turned towards her. She whispered, 'Remember our prayer? That the people who work on this film would be changed by it?'

'I sure do, Gwen,' I said. 'Thank you, Lord. Thank You, indeed.'

So it was clear to Gwen and me and to the people working on the film, that the most important concern for the movie was already being answered: the Gospel was being preached and even before the film was finished, people's lives were being changed.

It never once occurred to me that we could also pray for financial success.

The subject did not enter my mind later either, as the production was finished and plans made for a premiere.

I think I know the reason for my lack of awareness about something mundane like money. It was because I was so very, very aware of a situation much closer to my heart:

Jerry.

4

Homecoming for Jerry

Intercessory prayer is hardest of all when we are praying for the people we love most...

I HAVE TWO BROTHERS, Jerry and Don. Today Don works with me as the director of the New York branch of Teen Challenge, and is as close a friend as he was when we were children.

The person I want to talk about for the moment though is my other brother, Jerry. Jerry is two years younger than I. When we were kids I think this age difference bothered him, for he was always in my shadow. Mum and Dad tried to treat us equally, but when money was tight I somehow always got the new clothes and Jerry got the hand-me-downs: you can't pass clothes upward from younger to older.

Jerry was good-looking. He was robust — perhaps that was due to all those pints of ice cream he ate, listening to ball games on the radio. He was husky, not fat, for Jerry was a sports buff. He was into all the sports going, and he played them well. Whenever people came to the house they patted Jerry on the head and made some comment about what a fine-looking boy Dad had.

Then they looked at me.

There I sat with my ears too big, wearing horn-rim glasses, already looking gaunt. 'And I suppose little David is going to take after his Dad and be a preacher!' That was the world's reaction to me.

From early childhood Jerry and I were sent, every summer, to the old-fashioned 'Living Waters Youth Camp. I found a great identification listening to the camp preachers talk about the Second Coming and the Day the Trumpet would blow. When I was eleven and Jerry nine we were together at Living Waters one weekend when the theme was Total Commitment. That was the hour when God touched my heart. I ran down the sawdust trail — there actually was sawdust in the aisle — and knelt at the straw-strewn altar rail to give my life to the Lord.

I assumed that the whole world was going to be different after that. Jerry would be different too. But as a matter of fact my world didn't change much. Mother remained her collected self. Dad's duodenal ulcers continued to give him both fear and pain and left him keyed up emotionally. And Jerry, who had not gone down the sawdust trail with me, drifted more and more towards sports and away from things of God. I couldn't understand this, for to me the things of God were becoming more important every day.

The rift between Jerry and me got worse over the subject of Dad's discipline. Dad was a disciplinarian of the old school. He took quite literally the warning that to spare the rod was to spoil the child. No child of his was going to be spoiled. Whenever we were spanked it was I who kicked, screamed and yelled and Jerry who just dug his feet in and would not cry. Dad called it stubbornness.

'I'm going to knock that stubbornness out of you, son,' Dad said time after time, and he attempted to do just that with his leather belt. Jerry's response was always the same. He carried the hurt quietly within him.

When we were teenagers Jerry turned still more to sports and drifted further from Dad's spiritual teaching. The girls flocked to Jerry but they never seemed to look at me. Not only was I far from good-looking, skinnier and more near-sighted than ever, but not a one of the girls I liked could understand the kind of fantasy I indulged in. For all my dreams had to do with the church. I composed sermons in my mind, sermons that made people laugh or cry. When Dad found out about these imaginings, he chided me. 'David,' he said, 'why do you get so carried away?'

I don't think any one incident was responsible for the growing alienation between Jerry and me. Still, there was a watershed scene which accelerated things.

When I was seventeen and Jerry fifteen we both had jobs in the same grocery, Harkins' Market. I was the check-out clerk and Jerry the stock boy. I wanted so badly for Jerry to succeed that when he did something wrong I jumped all over him.

One day a customer gave Jerry $50.00 towards payment of a bill and Jerry lost the money. When I found out about it I called him a ne'er-do-well. In front of a store full of people, too. Jerry took his apron off and walked out of the store.

I realised that I had hurt him and ran down the street to see if I could make things right. But Jerry didn't even turn around. He went into a silence that was far more than a pout. From that day on Jerry seemed to shut me out of his life.

I suppose it is not unusual for a man to be so close to his brother that he fails to see change taking place. Jerry drifted away not only from me but from the family and I didn't even notice it until, one Sunday, I woke up. We were in church and Dad was preaching. For some reason my eye drifted sideways and I got a look at Jerry's face. He was listening, but I'd rather have seen him dozing. For Jerry's face registered distaste for what Dad was saying. He winced and shook his head, never openly enough to call attention to himself, but I knew. Jerry had moved into a different world.

After that Jerry began to make the break more obvious. I sensed a bitterness in him, a resentment at living in the pressure of a preacher's home. Jerry had already left. He became determined not to be 'forced into a mould' by Dad or Mom.

So Jerry and I moved still further apart. I went into the ministry, took up my work with alcoholics and drug addicts and gang members in New York. Jerry lived in Pittsburgh where he married Evelyn and at first seemed to be settling down well enough. He and Evelyn began a family and were happy in their suburban home. Jerry had a good job as produce manager in a supermarket in Pittsburgh. But I was so busy winning souls that I neglected to keep in touch with my own brother. I did not even know, until the day Mother came into my office with the news, that Jerry had started drinking.

I remember that day so clearly. Mother came in, quite agitated. She had just come back from a visit with Jerry and Evelyn.

'David,' Mother said, 'we must pray about Jerry. He is drinking. And I don't mean social drinking, either. If he's not an alcoholic right now, he's on his way.'

'Sure, Mother,' I said. 'Let's pray.' And of course we did. But to my shame I admit that by the end of the week

I was so busy that I had quite forgotten Jerry again. Work simply blotted his problem from my mind.

Over the next three years, Jerry's drinking got out of hand. He began staying away from his job and would spend hours drinking with the fellows. Finally, Jerry left home, ashamed to let his four children witness his 'falling apart'. It was a sad day for Eve and the kids.

'When I'm out drinking,' Jerry confided to Mother, 'I just can't think of my family. Alcohol consumes my time, my thinking, my entire existence.'

One Saturday evening at midnight the phone rang. It was Mother. She had been crying. 'David, I've just had a call-from Jerry. We've just got to pray for him quickly. He said he was going to kill himself.'

So then and there on the phone we prayed that Jerry come to New York where we could work with him. As soon as Mother hung up I went into the living-room determined that this time I was going to pray, really pray, for Jerry.

But I couldn't. The heavens were brass. It hit me that I had not spoken to him in months. I had been 'so busy' I had neither written him nor phoned him.

Over the next two hours I found myself under a terrible conviction. A verse of scripture came to mind: 'But if any provide not for his own, and specially for those of his own house, he hath denied the faith, and is worse than an infidel' (I Timothy 5:8).

That Saturday evening for the first time in my life I discovered what intercessory prayer is all about. I lay on the floor in our living-room and cried out to God, not caring how much noise I made. I determined to stay right there, not letting go of my search for the Lord until I knew that I had reached His heart. I prayed until three in the morning. I prayed remembering Dad's own death-bed petition, that not one of his children remain outside the Kingdom of God. 'Lord,' I said, 'please please bring Jerry to New York before he hurts himself further. Bring him here where we can work with him.'

A peace finally settled over me and I knew that God had heard. With an assurance that was really a Word of Knowledge I knew that soon Jerry would be sitting in this very same room.

The next day, Sunday, I was so confident that a call would come from Jerry that I did not go to church. Mother came by the house. Her puffy eyes betrayed the sleepless, tear-filled, prayer-filled night that she too had spent. With a word of encouragement from me that Jerry would soon be there, Mother went to church with Gwen and the kids.

At eleven o'clock the phone rang. I was not at all surprised to hear Jerry's voice. He was at the Port Authority building in Manhattan. 'Tell me how to get to your house, David; I want to see you.'

So I gave him directions. I told him I would meet him on the Staten Island side of the Narrows, and an hour later I was standing at the ferry slip wondering if I would even recognise my brother.

Three boats came and went and then, there he was. I saw him on the prow. He was unshaven and he seemed fifteen years older than when I had seen him last. His uncombed hair fell down into his eyes. My first thought was to thank the Lord that Dad didn't have to see this.

Then Jerry came off the boat. We couldn't find anything to say and finally just grunted to each other.

'Man, do I need a shave,' Jerry said.

'Okay.'

So we drove to Stewart Avenue where Gwen and I lived. I was deep in prayer. 'Jerry, whatever your plans are, don't make a move until you've talked to Mom.'

I got towels and an electric razor and showed Jerry where the bathroom was. I was so alarmed by my alcoholic brother that as he was showering I found myself on my knees again. I prayed out loud, not caring whether he heard or not.

The bathroom door opened and Jerry stepped across the hall and into our bedroom. A moment later I heard a thud. It sounded as if a body had fallen. 'Oh God,' I cried aloud, in the quickest of prayers. I flung the door open. There lay Jerry on the floor, but he was all right. He had simply tripped. He was crying.

We had a prayer meeting then and there.

Then I heard the front door open. Gwen, Mom and the kids came in.

'Mom, we've got company!' I called from the bedroom.

'Who is it, son?' she said, her tone clearly stating that she didn't want to talk with anybody.

'Come see.'

When she stepped through the door she let out a whoop of joy. Mom and Jerry were in each other's arms and we had another prayer meeting.

Then we really got serious. The next hour was one of the worst in my life, as we tried to get to the bottom of what had been happening.

Jerry was honest. 'Well, you may think it's silly, David, but I'll tell you anyway. At one store where I worked they sold books. *The Cross and the Switchblade* was one of the titles people kept asking for. The other clerks in the store wondered if I was one of *the* Wilkersons. That really made me feel lousy. I used to see you on the

Art Linkletter show and the Mike Douglas show. There you were out saving the world but you didn't care whether I lived or died.'

Jerry had built up a debt of three hundred dollars. This was just about the sum Gwen and I had put aside for a new rug. Now we looked at each other and we knew where that money should go.

The next day Jerry and I boarded a TWA flight for Pittsburgh. I had my chequebook with me. We rented a car and went to each of the places where Jerry owed money. The family paid his rooming house bill and his grocery bills. We cleaned up a bill at a clothing store. Then Jerry and I went to the north side and rented him another room. The most important thing was to find a church. We went to an Assemblies of God church near his room and introduced ourselves to the pastor. The pastor was understanding. 'Jerry, I'm here. Just call on me.'

The next thing was a job. We went back to the supermarket and found that they were happy to have Jerry back. When it was all over, Jerry said the nicest thing he had ever said to me,

'David, you're all right.'

'Well,' I said, 'you're all right, too, Jerry. The next hours are going to be important. You can either go on from here or you can go back to a bar and get smashed.'

Tragically, of the two courses Jerry chose the latter. I learned later from the Assemblies pastor that I had hardly taken off before Jerry was back in a bar. He came to the church once only. No, the pastor reported, he didn't know where Jerry was now. We wrote to the boarding house but Jerry had checked out leaving no forwarding address.

There was no longer anything we could do for Jerry directly. We could pray, though, and that's what we did with fervency. Mother especially never gave up. 'God's got His hand on that boy,' she said. 'We'll just have to pray him through.'

At Teen Challenge also not a day passed without serious intercession for Jerry. We couldn't reach him but he could reach us. Our prayer was for the day to come quickly when Jerry would contact us.

And finally he did. He showed up on the front steps of Teen Challenge, saying that he wanted to go through our programme. We took him in but two weeks later he ran off. Mother saw him once again, later, and decided to let him know where she stood on the whole affair.

'Jerry,' she said, 'we've done all we can. There is only one thing left now. To turn you over to Jesus. Come back when you're ready. Come on your own, not because anyone pressures you.'

Jerry walked out.

I got reports from people who said they had seen him wandering through the Bowery, a real bum now, living only to drink. Whenever I found myself driving through Manhattan, I somehow ended up in the Bowery looking, looking for Jerry. One time I stopped for a light. Men lolled around drunk: they curled up in doorways and on the sidewalk. Then I saw a man who looked exactly like Jerry. He was leaning over a garbage pail, vomiting. I pulled to the kerb and jumped out. The man stood up. It wasn't Jerry at all.

Our prayers mounted in intensity. Every day we prayed for my brother. Every night when we put the children to bed it was with the prayer, 'Dear Jesus, save Jerry.' And then later each evening when I went to my own midnight tryst with the Lord, I always, always spent time in intercession. 'Lord, You honoured the prayers of the importunate widow. Please let me be more importunate than she and listen to my plea.'

Then Pat Boone came to New York, to work on the movie. One day while we were on location in Harlem, I asked Pat, 'What are the chances of you and me conducting a crusade together at Glad Tidings?'

Pat was delighted. The only request he made was that we not advertise. Just word of mouth. I agreed, but unfortunately forgot to tell Pastor Berg at Glad Tidings about the understanding and he ran a small advertisement in the *Daily News*.

This 'accident' I know now was of God's design. For my brother read the advertisement.

Glad Tidings was packed out. Pat and Shirley Boone, Gwen and I were all down in the basement, getting ready to go upstairs, when my Crusade Director, David Patterson, came in.

'Guess who's here? Jerry!'

'You're kidding.'

'He's sitting in the last row, second from the left.'

'How does he look?'

'Awful.'

Shirley Boone was standing near-by. I told her briefly about Jerry and about the way we had finally relinquished him to the Lord. While I was talking, Shirley began to cry.

'I want to pray about Jerry,' she said. She spread her fingers and pressed them against her brow. I could see tears rolling down her dress. She prayed in the Spirit for a long time, then suddenly she reached out and took my sleeve. Her face was bright with joy. 'Don't worry,

David,' she said. 'God has answered your prayer. This night will be Jerry's homecoming.'

A sense of expectancy was mounting within me. We went upstairs. While Pat gave his testimony, I prayed for Jerry. My turn came. I stood up. I was just opening my Bible when I saw Jerry peeping around the people in front of him. I knew what I had to do.

'Folks, I'm going to ask your patience and prayers while I do something I have never done. Tonight I'm going to give an invitation to a single person.' I pointed to Jerry. 'It's either going to make him mad and he'll run out, or he will step this way and settle things with the Lord. Jerry,' I said, 'the last time we met I said you'd come back in your own way, when you were ready. Remember? Well tonight you have come back. Jerry, I'm calling to you in the name of the Lord. Make your decision to be on His side.'

By now everyone was turning to see who I was talking to. Suddenly a dishevelled old man jumped to his feet. He crawled over the person next to him and stood in the aisle. For just the briefest moment it was impossible to tell which way he was going to go.

But then — he ran towards me.

Literally ran. He threw himself to his knees and raised his hands. He shouted, 'I'm a rotten sinner. Save me, Lord Jesus.'

Pat knelt beside him. Pat prayed the sinner's prayer, the same starting prayer I had used so often. He asked Jerry repeat after him, 'Lord Jesus, I know that I'm a sinner...'

'Lord Jesus,' Jerry echoed. '. . . I know that I am a sinner.'

'. . . I know that You can take away my sins . . .'

'. . . I know that you can take away my sins . . .' Jerry said.

'. . . and forgive them right now.'

'. . . and forgive them right now . . .' We could barely hear Jerry's voice as he repeated the prayer after Pat. 'From this moment on I want to give myself to You. This is where I'm going to start. The rest is up to You.'

Everyone was crying now, the entire congregation, including Jerry, Pat, me, Shirley, Pastor Berg, Gwen.

Hours, centuries, later, when we went out together for a bite to eat, Jerry said to me, 'David, I know you're wondering whether this is just another one of my flash-in-the-pan changes. Well, it's not. I feel that way down deep. In the past I always held back five per cent of myself. But not now. Not this time, David. This time it's for life.'

We drove Jerry to Rehrersburg, Pennsylvania, where we have our rehabilitation farm. As the weeks passed we heard that Jerry was keeping late hours studying the Bible after all his farm chores were finished. His spiritual life developed rapidly. An attitude of praise came upon him. That was the thing I had been looking for.

One day I got a letter from Jerry saying, 'Dear David. Serving Jesus is better than *weiners, beans* and *apple sauce.*'

Weiners, beans and apple sauce had always been our very favourite dish at home. I found myself shouting for joy and giving the Lord praise too.

Six months later a group from Teen Challenge went to Pittsburgh; Jerry was with them. While in the area, Jerry telephoned his wife Evelyn and asked if he could see her and the children. Shortly, he was hugging and squeezing the children he had not seen in so many years.

His boy, Kenny, now twelve, put the question everyone was thinking, 'Hey, Dad. When are you coming home?'

So Jerry returned to his family. One day a call came to him from Delmar Ross, the Director of Teen Challenge in Cleveland. 'I need a travelling representative, Jerry. Would you consider coming to work for me?'

Several months later I had the honour of holding an evangelical meeting with my brother. It was a big success. Jerry introduced me and Evelyn and his children to some alcoholics he had brought to the Lord. Afterwards, in the parking lot, Jerry's boy, Kenny, looked at me and said.

'Thank you, Uncle Dave, for letting God use you to bring Dad home.'

As Jerry was going to pay the parking bill I whispered to Evelyn, 'Is he really changed?'

'He's really changed, David.'

Better than weiners, beans and apple sauce. Praise the Lord! Such a comment from Evelyn was surely better than weiners, beans and apple sauce for me. Jerry was home!

5

Living on the Edge of Expectancy

Money is one way to hear God's voice

WE WERE LEARNING so much in the days following the
appearance of *The Cross and the Switchblade*: the importance of having a trysting place, how to rely on the Lord's
timing, how to trust Him when it came to finances. . .

Or at least Gwen and I and the team at Teen Challenge
thought we had learned our lessons about money.

We were soon to find that we had not.

The movie became an instant success. With the exception of large sophisticated centres like New York, it
almost always played to packed houses. The film's success
was far more than box office numbers, for we were seeing
the answer to the very first prayer we had made on behalf of
the movie: 'Lord let this true adventure bring thousands
of people to You.' Day after day we were getting reports
that precisely this was happening.

But behind the scenes at Teen Challenge, something
else was happening. We began to get phone calls from
people who had seen the theatres packed to the four walls.
'Congratulations' the gist of the calls went. 'At least you
don't have any money problems, now that the royalties
are rolling in.'

Of course the cheques hadn't actually come in yet,
there is always a delay on royalty cheques. Nevertheless, in

89

our own hearts we were feeling that our money problems *were* over. We had finally found a hose that was connected to some hidden dollar pump, granting a steady supply of economic fuel. As soon as those royalty checks got here, I would no longer have to pray for money. What a relief! I could pray for the problems of people. 'Lord, thank You. It *is* better to pray for people than to pray for things.'

I even brought this attitude into our staff prayer meetings. 'It's going to be great to have money in the till. We won't need to scrounge any longer,' I pronounced confidently.

Everyone rejoiced with me. Everyone, that is, except Gwen. She spoke up very timidly with a word that turned out to be prophetic.

'It will never happen,' Gwen said. 'God does not intend for us to live without leaning directly on Him for our supply.'

Time passed. We should have been receiving cheques from Hollywood, but somehow there were more delays. Then, incredibly, within one single week we got two earthquake telephone calls.

The first was from Dick Ross. Ross called to say that he had had a lot of unexpectedly heavy expenses. Royalties we might earn could be delayed.

And then came the call from the attorney for Bernard Geis Associates. They had been slow in paying royalties, and we had not pressed. Now, the attorney said, Bernard Geis Associates was filing a petition in court for an arrangement under Chapter Eleven of the Bankruptcy Act.

Well, I came out fighting. 'It's not fair!' I found myself moaning to the Lord. 'I'm going to sue!'

I knew as a simple technical fact that my anger was not

based on greed. For all of my royalties from *The Cross and the Switchblade*, both book and film, had been assigned to the foundation which supports Teen Challenge. I drew my expenses and enough of salary to support our modest split-level house. That was all. The rest of the money was to be spent directly on hungry addicts and lonesome, needy kids. No, it wasn't personal greed. I had *righteousness* on my side — and I was going to sue!

But immediatly we discovered a few facts of life. Our attorneys warned us that it would cost $15,000 just to *start* such lawsuits. That was the beginning figure.

More importantly, once I had cooled down, the Lord gently but incisively dropped into my mind a few reminders about the Christian life. We were not to go to court with other believers. We were to be as wise as a serpent but as gentle as a dove, good stewards, but never fixing our hearts on the treasures of this world. In the end John and Tib and Gwen and I decided that we should go as far as possible to straighten things out without acting like belligerents. Then we should take seriously the Biblical injunction, 'Having done all, stand.' We would just pray and wait and see.

The outcome of all this deliberation was to realise that Gwen's prophetic statement had been correct: we were destined to depend directly on the Lord for our supply. As of this writing, the royalty funds are still either gone altogether or tied up in arrangement proceedings. It is possible that we may eventually get a partial settlement, but even then the money will probably just dribble in. There will likely be no huge lump sum to give us problems adjusting to the woes of the rich.

In many ways I think the Lord was protecting us at Teen Challenge by not having too much money come in as the result of our own efforts. The Lord had been dealing with us from the beginning on the subject of money. We were to live by faith. Perhaps some people could get away with establishing stewardship departments to manage portfolios. But for us, there was a risk inherent in this: we would become less dependent upon the Spirit. At the very last of *The Cross and the Switchblade* we said that the Holy Spirit was in charge here. If He really was in charge, He had to be in charge of our financial life, too.

The successes of the book and movie actually hurt us financially in an unexpected way. Many people stopped supporting us because they were under the impression that we were rolling in bank books. But as we were forced back into a dependence upon the Holy Spirit, we found we were living in a constant state of adventure again, sometimes even humorously.

One day we were faced with a vexing problem. We owed a large grocery bill. When I mentioned this to a friend (he didn't have any money, by the way) he was surprised. How could a well-established group like ours owe a large *grocery* bill! That sounded like the kind of problem a group of fledgelings might face. I explained our theory that it is wrong to build up extensive bank reserves. When money comes in, it goes out — feeding, housing, evangelising. We do not think of money as a reservoir to be held until needed, but as water-in-flow, working as water does in a hydro-electric plant.

So even today, just as in our earliest years, we are likely to find ourselves strapped, out of money, and food, etc., and faced with something as elementary as a grocery bill.

One day just exactly such a situation did arise. For

years we had been dealing with a wholesale grocer in New York, Stewarts, who had been very generous about extending us credit. But this time I knew we had gone too far. The bill which my secretary placed on my desk that morning was for more than a thousand dollars.

'Wow, how'd it get that high?' I asked.

'I think we'd better pray about it,' was her reply.

Which we did, during staff prayers. 'Lord Jesus,' we said quite simply. 'Here's this bill for one thousand dollars. We sure would appreciate Your taking care of it.'

Three days later we got an astonishing letter in the mail. The postmark read Baltimore, Maryland. There was an unsigned note inside which left us holding our sides with laughter. The note said:

'I've read your book, and I really like you. Will you please include me in your prayers. I play the horses. Pray that my horse will win!'

Well, two days later came another Baltimore letter, fat and bulky. Inside were stuffed $238! The unsigned note simply said, 'Thank you. Pray harder.'

And a few days later, still another envelope came. This time we counted $960. Again the unsigned note. This time it said, 'God sure answers prayer!'

We were just about choked with laughter. The problem remained, however: what were we going to do with the money? 'You're not going to spend it!' one of the staffers exclaimed. 'That's sin money!'

All right then, what were we supposed to do with it? If we had been able to send the money back, I'm sure we would have. Or we could donate it to some charity, thus giving *them* the problem of what to do with sin money.

That day in our prayers, we tried to find a scriptural

answer to the amusing dilemma and I think we found one.
When David went into the city of Nob he asked the priest
Ahimelech for five loaves of bread to feed his men, but
was told that there wasn't any common bread. Illegally,
David took holy shewbread from the priest and fed his men
(1 Samuel 21:1–6). Was the message of this experience
clear? Do we make a mistake when we put the words
holy or unholy on to supply. Supply comes from the Lord
and perhaps it is not up to us to tell Him what we will and
what we will not accept. In the end we came to see that
we had prayed for enough money to pay the grocery bill
and, with a wonderful wink, the Lord had given us the
money and at the same time nudged us not to be self-
righteous.

At Teen Challenge we have what may be a unique
practice. Whenever we are in need of encouragement we
present God with a bill. Quite literally.

We don't present every bill to the Lord, for most of the
time He takes care of our money needs as they arise. But
occasionally something will go wrong in our work: a boy
falls back on to heroin, or a friend says something hurtful,
or we feel we are overworked. At such moments we need
the encouragement of hearing from the Lord directly.
Are we on the right track? Do we need to stop and
regroup?

It is at these times that we present a bill to the Lord. We
bring the physical piece of paper into the prayer-room,
hold it up to the Lord and give it to Him to handle. 'Lord
Jesus, we've got this bill which we give to You. If we are
pleasing You, would You pay it quickly, please? Thank
You, Lord.' As simple as that.

One day we were feeling in particular need of an encouragement. We also had incurred a bill for $15,000.00 for a new heating system, and we wanted to pay it as quickly as possible. The combination seemed right.

'Lord,' we said at prayers, 'here we are again, needing to hear from You. Would You speak to us through this bill for the heating system? We request that You pay it to the dollar.'

Two days later, a letter came from a wealthy friend. Enclosed was a note, 'Dear Brother David. Please find herewith a donation. I feel that you have been praying for a need.'

My heart beat rapidly. 'Oh, boy,' I shouted out loud. 'Here it is! Thank You, Lord!'

I was a bit premature. When I unfolded the cheque it was for a hundred dollars.

'Thank You, Lord, just the same,' I said. And then I caught myself. What did I mean, 'just the same'. 'Thank You, Lord, very much indeed,' I said. And then I wrote the donor an especially warm letter of appreciation.

Two days after this my brother Don stepped into the office. He was excited.

'David, do banks make mistakes?'

'What do you mean?'

'Well, I've this cheque which I can't figure out. It's a bank draft from California and it's probably supposed to be for $14.90 or maybe $149.00. But the cheque reads $14,900. What an odd figure.'

Well, you could have heard me down the block praising God for that one. I was so curious about the timing that I placed a call to California to our donor, whom I did not know. He was surprised to hear from me.

'I just had to tell you a little about what your gift means

95

to us,' I said. 'We have a contractor's bill here for an even $15,000...' Then I told him how we had prayed for that money, how first a hundred had come in and then out of the blue arrives the cheque for $14,900. 'You can imagine how encouraged we are,' I said. 'But I just wanted to find out why you gave that peculiar amount.'

The fellow said he didn't really know. He said he had read about our work, that he had a business which had made a little money, and that he had decided to send us a cheque for $14,000. But as he was getting ready to write it out, the figure $14,900 kept coming into his mind. The experience was as encouraging to him as it was to us. All the way through our conversation he kept saying, 'Well what do you know? What do you know!'

We called this life-style of dependency upon the Holy Spirit 'Living on the edge of expectancy'. And we made it a point to tell the kids at Teen Challenge how we lived, because we early discovered that seeing specific answers to specific prayers is a faith builder.

One day a young girl came to 416 Clinton Avenue. We had never seen her before. She looked a little as if she were wearing the *costume* of a hippie instead of being for real — everything about her seemed extreme and somehow make-believe; hair dramatically long, fingernails dirtier than could have been possible without study, beads that reached to her knees.

Anyhow it happened that we were at prayer and we invited the young woman to join us.

We faced a problem at Teen Challenge. For we had been expanding rapidly. On Clinton Avenue alone we now used four buildings.

This created a peculiar kind of problem which centred

around equipment. For much of our washers and dryers and stoves and lawn mowers and automobiles were operated by converted drug addicts. Coming from city streets they tended not to know much about taking care of machinery and it seemed we were always having a breakdown.

In time we decided we were just going to have to buy a lot of new equipment. So we asked the kids to do some homework. What machinery needed replacement and how much would it cost?

It happened that on the day the results came in, our young over-dramatic hippie walked through the door. She listened, puckering her lips derisively as the kids read from their list.

'Lord, we need $216 for a clothes dryer in the women's dorm.'

'Lord, the new engine for the tractor on the farm, it says here, is going to cost $730. We pray for that.'

When the kids were through, the total of their requests came to more than $5,000.

I noticed that Miss Hippie slipped out towards the end of these prayers; I thought she had heard enough and had left. But in a few minutes she came back with her eyes slightly mocking. She stood at the front of the little chapel and told us how she had just called her father who was the president of a successful company in the South. She told him she was in desperate need of $5,000. Would he make the cheque out to Teen Challenge, and send it to 416 Clinton Avenue in Brooklyn? That same day, please?

'And he agreed.' She laughed. 'So there. It wasn't God who got your new clothes washer and mower and stuff at all. It was me!'

'Really?' The voice came from one of our ex-addicts; he was still on his knees.

'We thank you, of course,' he said. 'And your father too. Really. But let's not put down a miracle, huh? *You* were our miracle, praise God, coming in at just this moment.'

But the boy wasn't through. Getting up off his knees he walked to the front of the chapel where Miss Hippie stood. 'I know you,' he said, and when the girl looked startled he made it clear that he knew a lot of girls *like* her, rich, coming to New York as a protest against parents and finally getting into trouble.

The minute the boy said this, our friend began to cry. She told us that she had been walking the streets as a prostitute, she had been using drugs; she was desperate and lonesome.

'Then the real reason you came here today,' our ex-addict said, 'was not so you could help us. You were brought here by Jesus, so that He could find you. Do you see that?'

'Yes,' our friend said. The rest of the room was quiet as the two young people talked. Over the next half hour we watched the ex-addict lead the girl into a new relationship with the Lord.

Thanks to some broken piece of machinery, we witnesssed two miracles that day.

My mother used to keep a supply of coins and bills under her mattress.

It was a very special fund which she called her 'burden money'. Mother would give it to people whose names God laid on her heart. Over the years I have come to feel that this habit is a key to the secret of turning money into a blessing.

There were four characteristics of Mother's burden money. First of all it was not her tithe; she and Dad continued to tithe to their local church wherever they lived; the burden money was above and beyond tithes, money she managed to save out of her household funds.

Secondly the money had a specific purpose: it was used to *encourage*.

Thirdly, the money only went to missions. This was a word Mother used broadly. Anyone working to spread the Good News was missionary as far as Mother was concerned. Thus, if a milkman used his job to teach Jesus he was a missionary, and might easily receive a surprise 'gift from the Lord as an encouragement'.

And last, Mother never gave her burden money away except where she was specifically instructed to do so during her prayer time. I once asked her how this worked. 'Well,' she said, a little startled that I should pose such a basic question, 'you simply ask the Lord which person. He wants to encourage today and He always tells you.'

Not long ago our staff was on a crusade. We were talking about Mother's burden money and someone made the suggestion:

'Why don't we take part of the money we had planned to spend on ourselves and give it away. Each morning we will ask the Lord, "God, please show me specifically who You want to encourage today."'

Within a week we were getting interesting reports.

One wife of a staff member said that while she was visiting friends, she met a missionary. As they talked she 'knew' that she should give this man a gift from the Lord.

When an opportunity came, she pulled him aside and handed him five bills.

'This is for you,' she said. 'The Lord has told me to give it to you.'

The missionary's hands shook as he took the money. 'You just can't know what this does for my faith,' he said. 'I'll be honest with you: my wife and I didn't know . . . well, tonight we would have gone hungry.'

Nearly everybody in the group had a story like that. The Lord always made it clear who should get the money and all of us could report encouraging little, homey miracles, if such a phrase could be used.

I have followed Mother's example too: Gwen and I have opened a separate bank account which we called 'Missions'. As with Mother, that's very a loose term. It could mean home missions or foreign missions and it can mean individuals who are working for God. The very first day I opened this account I asked the Lord to supply the name of a person He wanted to encourage. He did it in a most interesting way. He told me to open the Directory of Missions put out by our church. Then he told me to let my finger run down the directory page.

All of a sudden one name seemed to leap out. It was of a man I had never heard of; he was working in Arizona among the Indians. I had the impression that I should send him $200. Along with the cheque I wrote a note, 'You don't know me, but I feel that the Lord has told me there is something you need. So I'm sending you this cheque. It's God's way of telling you, "I know all about you and I know about your needs."'

Later I got a letter back filled with explanation points and hallelujahs. 'This may be hard to believe,' he said, 'but we have been praying specifically for $200. We want it for a down-payment on a very much needed pick-up truck. We are so astonished at the pinpoint way God has met this need that we are greatly encouraged in all our work. Thank you. And praise the Lord!'

I am convinced that this is one way that God would have His Church's financial needs met.

He would much rather, it seems to me, work mystically than through the bureaucracy of large funding campaigns.

Every opportunity I get now, I encourage people to start a burden money fund of their own. Recently a millionaire friend came to me with a fairly typical complaint. 'I don't think my money is going in the right direction, David,' he said. 'Do you have any suggestions?'

'Well, to start with, don't give the money to us,' I said, 'not unless the Lord Himself tells you to do so.' Then I told him about the burden money idea. 'Why not open a missions account? Start with $1,000. As the money is used up, add to the fund again. Go to the Lord every day with the same prayer, "Lord, lay someone on my heart this day. Be specific, please. Is there someone You want to speak to through money?"'

A few days later this friend contacted me again. 'David, do you know what I've discovered? All these years I have never known what it was to be blessed, *myself*, in giving. I only gave because I thought I ought to. I never knew what it was to sanctify the gift in prayer.'

To sanctify the gift, that's the idea. To put giving into a framework of prayer and let the Lord send money where He wills. He knows the need. We don't. Like all rich people, this particular millionaire was faced with a constant flow of worthwhile demands. How was he to decide where money should go? By following the burden money principle and depending on the Lord, giving became a blessing for both the giver and the receiver. 'It opens a whole new realm of praise,' the man told me.

Just imagine what it would be like if we really could get away from dependence on organised giving. For one thing salaries and overhead often takes sixty per cent of the money before it ever gets to its destination. (Our work, by the way has an overhead cost of less than twenty per cent) For another, the mystery and excitement of receiving and giving, input and output is gone. Suppose we are to have a pool of people, a hundred thousand Christians around the world, who would say, 'Jesus, my ears are open, my heart is open, my pocket is open. Lead me to a mission that is in need.' No longer would we be giving — or receiving — in a perfunctory way. We would plug into the world's needs. And we would be living in a constant flow of miracles; time and again people will write back saying something like, 'How on earth did you know that I needed exactly $35?'

My wife Gwen has a rather unusual variation on the burden money fund. She says it's all right to remember missions, but don't forget the missionary. So she gives dresses away. She manages in one way or another to find out the dress size of our missionary wives and then out of the blue she'll send a bright, pretty costume. I wish Gwen had kept the letters she has received expressing joy and lifted spirits. I have picked up her idea too, and have a deal worked out with a local haberdasher where it's possible to buy a really good suit for $88. If a missionary comes through — and the Lord lays his need on my heart — I hand him a card and ask him to go to the store to pick out a suit. 'The gift is from the Lord,' I say, 'to remind you that He cares about things like clothes.'

A pool of a hundred thousand men and women. A pool that prays, 'Lord, this day show me what mission or missionary I should give money to, above and beyond my tithe.' What a blessing flow that would be!

So since *The Cross and the Switchblade* money continues to be a blessing for us. I don't mean that we've been blessed by *having* a lot of money, because the Lord has seen to it that this has not happened. But I do mean that money still is a wonderful way of hearing from Him. When we always live by faith, no matter how much money passes through our stewardship, when we constantly bring Jesus into every money decision, and especially when we become part of God's mystic supply for His Church, when we do these things then we are truly letting money be a blessing.

6

The Day I Quit the Rat Race

Have you ever felt swamped . . . ?

MOST OF THE WORK begun at the time *The Cross and the Switchblade* was written has matured reasonably well.

At least it seemed that way.

By looking at the figures, we were doing all right. And a lot of people kept telling me that the proof of the pudding was in the statistics.

Take for example the five buildings we owned on Clinton Avenue alone. They were all badly needed. Some were dormitories. Others were screening centres where we weeded out kids who were not serious about changing their way of life. One building was set aside for administration.

Then there was the rehabilitation farm in Rehrersburg, Pennsylvania. Soon another followed, in Missouri. And then another, in California. And another, in Canada.

We had developed a rather unusual method for expanding the work of Teen Challenge. We grew by encouraging independent ministries. I didn't feel that even the name Teen Challenge belonged to us, so I encouraged other people to borrow our principles and the name itself for use in their own local situation. Our role would be to advise, pray, and help raise funds. Beyond that the work was up to the local Spirit-anointed churches in any community.

So it was that an ex-addict started a centre in Puerto Rico, a feed salesman began Teen Challenge in Los Angeles; many new centres were organised by local churches in just about every state in the Union. The Idea worked beautifully. Before we knew it, there were forty-six centres in the United States and Canada and we were ready to leap overseas.

The overseas vision saw even faster growth than our work at home. In 1969 a young man named Howard Foltz who had founded Teen Challenge in the Dallas–Fort Worth area came to me with the idea of moving into Europe. He went with my blessing and support and within two years there were more than fifty Teen Challenge centres and rehabilitation farms in Europe from Norway to Italy.

So now we were a world-wide network of interlocking fellowships. We had no central chain of command. We were not an organisation but an organism consisting of people who felt the same burden. Each leader of the now nearly a hundred centres around the world was a simple man like myself, and like myself, a man who depended upon the Lord.

Of course numbers did not tell the real story. That could only be seen in terms of changed individual lives. Our way of reaching these individuals remained basically the same. We would send workers into the street, into the shooting galleries where boys and girls were sticking needles filled with heroin into their arms. If a kid seemed interested we would invite him to the Centre for prayer. Of the ones who gave their lives to the Lord, either on the streets or at the Centre, most stayed on for our programme. They lived with us, taking a bed at Teen

Challenge. Then followed an intensive, disciplined, rigorous course of physical, moral and spiritual upbuilding. If a boy or girl got through the programme at all — and many dropped out — he had been so completely re-orientated to serving the Lord that there was an eighty per cent chance that he would remain clean.

Well, that was success, I guess. All those buildings. All those invitations to speak. All those top-name television personalities asking me to appear on their shows — Art Linkletter, Mike Douglas, Virginia Graham, Merv Griffin, the Tonight Show, the Today Show. We were very well accepted in rehabilitation circles, we had access to jails and hospitals and courts of the city. Psychologists and government workers came knocking on our doors to see what we were doing. I even had an invitation to appear before a prestigious medical society to present my findings. I knew how to talk the lingo of the profession now and I was well accepted at this conference. It made me feel pretty important.

All this growth called for funds. As each new Teen Challenge centre sprang up, it had to have money. I would fly into Chicago or Memphis or Oshkosh, speak before a group of a few thousand and with one appeal raise enough money for the programme to be launched. This was heady stuff. There seemed to be no limit to what I could achieve. Of course I tried to do all this in the Spirit. And certainly I maintained my nightly prayer vigil. But somehow I always seemed to be causing sparks to fly. I was living in a cyclone of activity. There were building plans to be approved. There were requests to start new centres. There were invitations to speak. There were desperate requests from parents.

And I tried to answer every call —

Oh, there were moments when I glimpsed the truth that I was not living within the peace of the Lord. When the Chinese man met me on the street in front of the Teen Challenge Centre, I learned that I had to keep a simplicity of faith within a complexity of life. But how I wondered if that were enough. Was it possible that my busy life itself was not of the Lord's making?

The experience which caught me up short was Kids Town.

What is there in man, I wonder, that makes him want to build ideal cities? Separated places of refuge. Utopias where all will be well.

Kids Town was my variation on this theme. I conceived an idea and the Lord simply didn't stop me. I had a dream, but not a mandate. And it wasn't until later that I discovered the difference.

Kids Town was going to be a refuge for all the troubled young people I was meeting. It would be located on a 150-acre tract of land, right next to Disney World in Orlando, Florida. Preliminary studies showed that building the basic campus would cost $8,000,000. *That* would really stretch my faith. A country boy raising $8,000,000, think of it!

We took an option on the land, and spent $5,000 drawing up preliminary plans, laying out roads and buildings on paper. If my so-loyal staff in New York seemed a bit reluctant to drain their efforts away from our street work in order to look at still another set of building plans, they hid their emotions well. Or else my spiritual ears were blocked and I did not catch the note. Kids Town was a boom town. Trust the Lord and away!

Although I did not realise it at the time, I wanted Kids Town so badly that I was afraid to pray for it. Since then I have come to place high value on this simple criterion: am I doing something that I brush over lightly in prayer? If so, the chances are I'm afraid to hear what the Lord has to say. I am moving in my own strength and not in the Lord's. I know that with Kids Town this is what I was doing.

But then one day an extraordinary thing happened.

I had said goodbye one more time to Gwen and the children, hopped aboard a jet paying no attention to my fear of aeroplanes and headed for Chicago. There, waiting for me, was a group of 10,000 people. I would tell them about the latest move of the Lord, how He was building His city-of-refuge in beautiful Florida right next to Disney World.

Only it didn't work that way.

Suddenly, just before I was to begin my presentation, the Lord dealt with me. It was swift and incisive. There, sitting on the platform, I felt sick at my stomach. I suddenly saw what I really was, a public relations man. An apologist for Jesus Christ before medical groups and conventions of psychiatric social workers. In His beautiful and gentle way, the Lord dropped into my heart the words, 'David, I did not call you to be a fund raiser.'

I shuddered. The man next to me leaned over and whispered, 'Are you all right?'

'Very all right, thank you.'

Again words came to my heart. 'You can't institutionalise everybody, David.'

And I knew it was so. Even if we were to build facilities to take care of thousands, it would still be like trying to empty the ocean with a teacup.

That evening, there on the stage, I made a promise, 'Jesus, as soon as I get home I'm going to lay hands on the horns of the altar.' This was a principle my grandfather taught me. It was based on the story of Adonijah who tried to take the throne away from King David. The scheme failed and Adonijah was now very fearful. He went into the Holy of Holies and grabbed hold of the two horn-like protrusions on the altar, declaring that he would remain there until he had an assurance of mercy for his stupidity. Grandfather knew that in every life there comes an hour when we try to take the kingship away from God: we want to put ourselves on the throne. When this happens and we finally wake up to what we have done, we should go into our own Holy of Holies, 'lay hold of the horns of the altar' and not leave until we have put the relationship back in its proper order.

I saw that night in Chicago that I had attempted to make myself king of my life, and I knew I had to do something about it. That same evening, instead of talking about Kids Town, I preached a simple message about finding the peace of the Lord by humbling yourself at His Cross. I was preaching to myself. When I finished and turned to sit down I noticed David Patterson, our Crusade Director, giving me a long, steady look. He was puzzled.

'It's all right, Dave,' I said. 'I know who the King is...'

'Praise the Lord,' Dave whispered.

The next day on the way home our plane hit turbulance. Once again I knew I had not conquered my old fear of flying. But I prayed out loud, 'Jesus, don't let this plane crash, please. I've got something I must straighten out first.'

Dave smiled. 'I think He'll give you the time, Brother Dave.'

And finally there I was, in our garage at home. At midnight I stretched out the black leatherette recliner in my prayer-room, I reached out my hands and imagined that I was another subject in another Holy of Holies, grabbing hold of the two projections that came out from the side of the altar, horns as it were. Jesus, here I am. And here I stay until I receive a new touch as Your servant.'

A peace swept over me, very similar I am sure to the peace that Adonijah felt when he knew he had a second chance.

After a while I began to ask the Lord what He wanted me to do with my life. In the silence of my prayer-room I began to hear some answers.

In the first place I must learn to *abide in my calling*. That is, I should stay in the work the Lord had called me to do, and not turn to something else.

My calling was in the person-to-person ministry. How my heart raced as the Lord showed me this. I was supposed to be working with people! Not that institutions were bad: certainly there were men who were called to build them. But not I. We should not dissolve the work of Teen Challenge, for certainly it had its place, but my own primary work should not be with the institution.

The second major thing that the Lord showed me that night was the difference between *general direction and specific direction*. It was not enough for me to be headed vaguely in a direction in my work for the Lord, towards a destination off in the distance somewhere that was not very clear. What He wanted me to do, instead, was to work quite close to Him, following specific day by day, hour by hour instruction: 'Turn right, turn left there. Do this, don't do that.'

'All right, Lord,' I said. 'Let's begin right now. I want to lay out, for You to examine, every single one of the projects I am involved in.'

I began with Kids Town. I asked the Lord if He wanted me to go on with that project. I was astonished at the swift, clearcut answer:

'Absolutely not!'

I argued a little. Not very seriously. 'What about the $5,000 we have spent on the plans, Jesus? That will just go to waste.'

And again the swift answer. 'The lessons you will learn are worth much more than $5,000! Besides, you never asked Me to show you the true motivation for Kids Town. Do you want to know now? You wanted to build a monument to yourself.'

Uhmm. I recognised this truth instantly. 'Lord, never, never, let me fall into that trap again, please.'

At about three o'clock that morning I began to get sleepy. I knew from experience that this was the Lord's way of telling me I should rest now.

When I got up off my leatherette recliner I knew that a whole new way of life had begun for me. I felt like a bird that had just been released from its cage.

I went into the house singing and I woke up the next morning with my heart still free. The first thing I did was to tell Gwen. She threw her arms about me. 'This sounds real good, Dave,' she said.

Just before they got off to school, I told the children of my plan to drop Kids Town. I wouldn't have to take that trip to Florida after all. Gary let out a whoop. He raced through the backyard and vaulted over the fence shouting to his buddy next door, 'Daddy's going to be home! Daddy's going to be home!'

When I got to the office that day, I called the staff in. I told them what had been happening to me.

'What would you think,' I said with trepidation, for

everyone had been working so loyally on the plans, '. . . what would you think if we dropped Kids Town?'

To my astonishment, everyone in the room started to praise the Lord. A new sense of freedom and peace settled over our staff from that day.

Nor was the Holy Spirit through with me yet. Again that night in my Quiet Time, I asked the Lord if there were something else He wanted me to get rid of. I lay out before Him every single meeting, every crusade which I had planned.

'What should I do about these?' I asked.

The answer came with unbelievable swiftness. 'Cancel them.'

'But, Lord, all those people are counting on me.'

'Cancel them. You are too structured. I want you to learn how to quit struggling.'

And that was all the Lord would tell me that night. Learn how to quit struggling? What could He mean? Was it possible that I had moved into a kind of spiritual rat-race?

The next day I did start the long process of paring down. It was surprising how nearly everyone I called understood instantly. 'Of course,' they said. 'We're sorry, naturally, but maybe the Lord will make it possible for you to come later . . .'

Every day, every hour now I could ask the Lord, 'What is it, Jesus, that You want me to do now?'

The Lord told me He wanted me to take a year-long sabbatical. I began to walk the streets again, as in the old days. I preached only when the Lord told me to preach, not because it filled my calendar and made me feel wanted.

Through it all I had an amazing freshness.

I spent the long days wandering in and out of back

streets talking with drug addicts, approaching alcoholics, meeting people in hallways and launderettes. At the end of these days I was fresher than when I started. It reminded me of a crusade I held once with Kathryn Kuhlman. I asked her how she maintained her vigour. 'It's the Spirit, David,' Kathryn said. 'There's your answer. He is the quickener, the enlivener. When you work under the anointing, you work under power and life.'

Well, that's the way it was with me. Gwen once actually asked me if I had taken the day off. 'You look so . . . you look almost . . . younger!'

And that's the way I felt, too. After supper I went out and played ball with the kids. I hadn't done that in ages.

The next day I was right back on the Lower East Side again, living out my new life. I moved with the Spirit. When He told me to talk with this person, pray for that person, I did. I found that He was breaking me away from dependence on our rehabilitation programme. He was teaching me to explore new areas of hope. Always before, I felt I had to bring every addict into the rehabilitation programme. Now I asked the Lord first. A few He had me bring to the Centre. The rest though, by far the majority, He had me turn over to local Spirit-anointed prayer groups and churches. It was the beginning of a new method of work.

After I had worked in this way for several weeks, the Lord allowed me to speak now and then to slightly larger groups. I began occasionally to accept a crusade. The Lord showed me that He wanted me to pray carefully over each invitation. As requests came in I put the information on three by five cards. These I would let accumulate for a while, then during my midnight prayer time I would put the cards on a table before me. 'Lord, do

You want me to go here?' I would pray. 'Or here?' Almost always the Lord said no. Occasionally, though, He would say, 'Yes, I do want you to go there.'

So it was that one morning I got a clearcut direction from the Lord to accept an invitation to Chicago. And with it began a new part of my walk with the Lord. For in Chicago He showed me that I was to be faced with the toughest mandate of my life.

7

Drugs in the Suburbs

We began to discuss the horror of. . .

THE LORD WAS SHAKING me up. And I still wasn't sure what direction I was supposed to take.

I only knew that He was calling me away from an over-structured life and away from projects where I was in danger of finding myself on the throne. Take no speaking date, plan no crusade that wasn't specifically given me in prayer, that seemed to be the rule.

Bit by bit even the size of our staff reflected this paring down. As we took fewer meetings and stopped spinning so fast, our workers could hear more clearly God's plan for their own lives. Some moved on to other work. One was my friend John Benton who had been helping me on crusades: John told me that for years God had been whispering to him and his wife, 'Start a rehabilitation centre for addicted girls.' He wanted to do that now. And so began the Walter Hoving Home for Girls in Garrison, New York.

And all the while the Lord seemed to be pulling me towards some as-yet-unseen new goal.

I got a glimpse of the new goal towards the end of a visit to an old friend who lived in Chicago. For years Al supported my work among young drug addicts in the slums of New York. Now we were saying goodbye just before my return to the East.

'Before you go, Dave,' Al said suddenly, 'I wonder if you could — I mean — it's our son Jimmy. He's been so kind of withdrawn lately. Nothing serious. Just part of being a fifteen-year-old.'

Of course I was glad to talk with Jimmy. And so I started up the stairs, not dreaming that at the top of them lay a glimpse of the future.

As of that night, in early 1964, I'd been working with drug problems for six years and I figured I knew all about the teenage user. He came from a rat-infested cold-water flat where there were too many children, too little money, too much defeat. He'd long since dropped out of an over-crowded school; drugs were his escape from a world that had left him behind.

The voice behind the door said, 'Come in!' to my knock, so I did. I stepped over some hi-fi equipment, avoided a weightlifting set, a twelve-string guitar and some bowling shoes. It wasn't easy, so thick was the eye-watering haze of marijuana.

Jimmy was sitting on the bed, a tall blond boy with eyes as hostile as any I had ever encountered on a Harlem street corner. 'My Dad sent you up here, didn't he?' were his first words.

I moved a cashmere jacket and some soiled socks off a chair and sat down. 'Maybe he sent me because you don't talk to him.'

'Don't talk! He doesn't listen, you mean.'

Suddenly at the prospect of having someone there who would listen, Jimmy dropped his air of hostility and began to talk. He told me he'd started drinking at thirteen. ('I like grass better because you don't throw up.') By fourteen he was taking 'ups' (amphetamines) in the morning and 'downs' (barbituates) at night; the dosage had tripled in the past year. The newest thing in his crowd was LSD: no one he knew had ever had a bad trip — he told me that was all propaganda. Finally it was I who had to break off the conversation to catch my plane.

As we drove to the airport I groped for the best way to tell my friend Al what I had learned. Maybe there is no good way to tell a father his young son is on the marijuana and barbituates trail. Al flew into a rage. He accused me of being deranged on the subject of drugs, of having worked with 'bums and street rabble' so long I didn't know a normal kid when I met one, and a lot more. He deposited me and my suitcase at the terminal and roared away and although I never saw Al again, it was far from the end of the incident. This was the beginning of the new phase of my work, a phase which was to over-shadow in size and complexity anything I had dreamed of.

For now that my eyes had been opened, I began to see these kids everywhere. Even at our own youth rallies around the country — whether in Los Angeles, Detroit, Hartford, Miami — there they were, usually a group of them and obviously to anyone familiar with the symptoms, on some kind of drug-induced high.

Afterwards, I'd talk to them, often sitting in the car they'd come in or in some carpeted dim-lit restaurant where I was glad they had charge accounts because I'd have hated to see the bill. Like Jimmy, they were willing, even eager, to talk. They introduced me to a whole new world of chemical and artificial drugs, far larger than the limited repertory of the slums. In six years I counted thirty-two different kinds of pills alone with nicknames that were the same all over the country: 'blue jackets', 'bennies', 'footballs', 'Christmas trees'. I met things you smoke, sniff, chew, inhale and inject. For some of these activities wondrous mind expanding effects were claimed. For others I could not make out that any positive experience was even hoped for. The most baffling to me was a substance called '68' concocted by kids in suburban New Jersey, which produced an epileptic-like fit lasting three days. Those kids I talked to who had not tried it were eager to. These were the days when Timothy Leary seemed to be the hero of every undergraduate with his urging of young people to drop out and goof off. Students began making acid in laboratories for their own use. The Maffia was discovering and quickly exploiting the huge, rich reserve of suburban wealth. Soon new words appeared: Horse, H., Smack.

Drug addiction, in short, was moving into the suburbs, needle and all.

Like Jimmy, the kids I met rarely treated drug information as confidential or asked me not to tell their parents. And so I tried to tell parents. I talked to school authorities, ministers, teachers. And it was Chicago all over again. I was an alarmist. Few adults were willing to consider the possibility that drugs might be a national — as opposed to an inner-city — problem.

But I had to believe what my own eyes were telling me. And looking ahead, I believed something else too. I believed that sooner or later some of these same bright, attractive kids with their sports cars and charge accounts, would be knocking at the door of 416 Clinton Avenue, Brooklyn. I had not, in 1964 — nor for several years after that — met a single middle-class heroin user. But I knew from our work in the slums that the road which starts with marijuana leads for many to this most final of all dead ends. Not every guy who puffs a joint goes on to shoot heroin into his veins of course — and not one ever believes that he will — but the observable fact is that many do. I knew that one day we would be getting these kids — 'goodniks' we called them, because they had so many of the good things our society has to offer — at our Teen Challenge home.

That day came in 1967. At first the boy, Bill, looked like any other ragged down-and-out junkie. He was crouched in the corner of a fire-gutted tenement in the Bronx, a building we always checked in our weekly swing through sections of the city where addicts hang out. Bill was coatless: an addict keeps a coat only long enough to pawn it. He hadn't eaten in so long he was unable to stand without help, yet when we suggested taking him for a meal he turned us down. A friend was working an angle for a fix and he wanted to be there when the friend got back. That wasn't what surprised me; I'd have been surprised at any other answer from a mainline heroin user. What turned my blood cold was *how* he said it. For out of this emaciated, dirty, sore-covered figure in front of me came the voice of an educated young man.

I knew better than to argue. I simply left him our card with the address of the Centre on it, told him that God loved him, and that there was food and a bed any time he needed it.

Two weeks later, Bill arrived at Clinton Avenue. From the start he was something new in our experience. Usually addicts arrived with one thing on their minds, to kick heroin. Bill, however, said very little about his drug problem, though he had a big and expensive habit. He talked about wonder cures that were on the verge of discovery and about important doctors who were friends of his father. When he spoke of his family, whom he had not seen in nearly a year, it was in terms of his father's income and the things that they owned. Through it all I couldn't help remembering Jimmy in Chicago, sitting in that bedroom surrounded with 'things'.

We got in touch with Bill's parents and had a second new experience: middle-class parents reacting to hard-core addiction. These fine, conscientious people showed remarkably little interest in the current situation, desperate as it was. Their attention focused on the past, on trying to assign blame – to the school, to a traumatic experience, to a fall from a bicycle – for what happened. They went over and over the events of Bill's childhood, stressing what they had given him: the flute lessons, the summers at camp, the costly years at the orthodontist. They seemed to want to impress us with the fact that they were not to blame – though this was the last thing we thought or cared about – constantly mentioning an older brother who had turned out well. 'Bill got in with the wrong crowd,' was their final conclusion. Although we had a strict rule against leaving the Centre until the first phase of withdrawal was complete, they pressed us constantly and unsuccessfully to make exceptions in Bill's case.

And meanwhile, other 'Bills' were finding their way to Clinton Avenue. On the night, years earlier, when I went up the stairs to Jimmy's room in Chicago, the average age of the addicts at the Centre was twenty-four. They came almost exclusively from three areas of New York City: Harlem in Manhattan, Bedford-Stuyvesant in Brooklyn, and 'Little Korea' in the Bronx; they were black or Puerto Rican.

Just six years later, over half the population at the Centre were white kids from the suburbs beyond the city, from the nicest neighbourhoods in town, and from out of state. There were so many fourteen- and fifteen-year-olds, among them, that our average age at Clinton Avenue was now closer to eighteen.

But there was a difference bigger than race and age and background, and that was in the ability to accept responsibility for a problem. Confused as he may be about life in general, the slum boy was very clear on one point: no one was going to do him any favours. He was usually a veteran of many jailings, of shrieking, sweating withdrawals on cold cement floors, of the relentless search for a fix starting again the moment of release. In those cells with him were hopeless old derelicts in whom he saw himself if he didn't succeed in breaking the cycle. If it occurred to him that society or his parents or the school system was responsible for his plight, he shrugged: however he got this way it was his problem now and nobody was going to make it disappear for him.

The suburban boy and his parents seemed to have a completely different set of premises. We'd never heard about a 'wrong crowd' until we met Bill's family: but we've heard about it from every set of middle-class parents since. They came to the Centre hoping we had the answer. If we didn't, there are other places that might. Every one of these families had influential friends, every one believed that somewhere, somehow, if they spent enough money, if they travelled far enough, if they consulted enough experts, they'd find a system that works.

But I knew nothing about systems. In thirteen years of working with addicts we had never found a technique that cures, though on many long nights of prayer we had begged for one. We didn't know what cured addiction;

but we knew Who did. Jesus Christ could heal heroin addiction. We'd seen it over and over again.

And this was what the new kind of addict seemed to find hardest of all. You see, Bill didn't make it. Fourteen months after he first came here, after entering and leaving our progamme several times, he was found dead of an overdose on a rooftop in Harlem. They searched his dirty clothes and found only one piece of identification, a card from Teen Challenge. It was my difficult task to call his parents. They didn't want to come to the morgue.

'You knew him, Rev-ren,' the father said. 'Help us out, won't you? If there's any charge of course we'll . . .'

'Yes. Well I'll let you know.'

Even after they had replaced the sheet I stood there in that bleak morgue, numb with bewilderment. Why did this happen to a boy like this? How did he get started? What did he need? What could we have done to help him?

That day I had none of the answers. But I did realise that I was up against some of the toughest problems of my life. Drug abuse in the suburbs was just beginning, but I *knew* that within months it would be headline news. There would be an increase of thrusts on the part of professional, heartless men ready to pluck these golden suburban apples as quickly as possible. Using our old methods we would never be able to keep up with the explosion of addiction. 'You can't institutionalise everyone, David,' the Lord had said to me. Now, more than ever, I saw what He meant. The old way of doing things just was not flexible enough. It must be more than buildings and beds and budgets, places and staffs. These were needed, to be sure; and I would go on being active in Teen Challenge ministries. But there was something new on the horizon. I could feel it.

Again I took to my knees: I didn't seem to be able to move without those midnight sessions.

'Lord Jesus,' I said. 'You have a plan. I know it. But what? The Maffia drug trafficker is just moving too fast for us.' I thought: In every city in the country, right this moment, the Maffia is out recruiting. He gets a kid hooked to a habit beyond his means. Then that boy has to hook three or four others, so that he can sell to them and support his own habit. The progression of addiction is astounding. If one boy hooks three, and each of these hooks three, and so on, by just eight progressions *more than 2,000 kids are addicted* . . .

I fell forward on to my face on the recliner. 'That's too much, Lord. Too much. Yet I know You have a plan. Show me, please. Show me quickly, Lord.'

When He in fact *did* show me, the answer came from such an unexpected direction that I almost didn't hear it.

One day I was working on the streets of the lower East Side in Manhattan. It seemed a little quieter than usual. I was expert now spotting the pusher, expert too at picking out the kids revved up on speed or goofing on heroin.

And they weren't there. At least they weren't in evidence.

Accidently, I found myself in the middle of a street stickball game. The small hard rubber ball was hit right to me and for once in my life I caught it! As a boy I had played scores of games with my brother Jerry, games that were ruined because I could never hold on to the ball.

But on this morning as the black boy's broomstick smacked the ball and it in turn smacked the palm of my hand, I looked down and there was the ball. I had caught it!

Well, I was an old enough hand to know a miracle when I saw one, and to wonder what I was supposed to do now. I just started talking. Still holding the ball, I said it looked like the Lord had given us an introduction, that I was a preacher working over in Brooklyn with kids strung out on speed and horse and alcohol and that I couldn't help noticing that there seemed to be fewer junkies around these days.

'I don't know about Brooklyn, Man,' the boy with the broomstick said. He placed it across his shoulder and ambled over. 'But down here the word's out. Speed kills.'

What did he mean. Who put the word out in this new way? Doctors, government, statistics, school health teachers had been saying this for years. I decided not to ask that obvious question straight out.

'And H? What about H?'

The boys laughed. Again it was the batter who answered. 'You must be crazy, Man. That ain't cool. For one thing I don't want no Brown Beret beating on me.'

Well, that's as far as I got that morning. The boys didn't want to talk any more, so I tossed my miracle ball back to them, wished them well and walked on down the litter-strewn street.

It wasn't until several hours later that I realised what I had just heard. These kids were scolding *me* for suggesting that they might be using hard drugs.

What was up?

Immediately I set out on something of a detective story

chase. I had two pieces of information. 'The word was out,' a new word from someone the kids listened to. And the Brown Berets were somehow involved. What would this group of militants have to do with drugs?

Using my two pieces of information, I went back down to the suspicious, hostile, lower East Side, and to Little Korea in the Bronx, and to the edges of Harlem — as far in as I dared go by myself — and asked sidewise questions. The results were very, very interesting.

First off, the militant Puerto Ricans and blacks in New York had taken a strong stand on drugs. Drugs made new slaves. Pushers and even users were spit on, scorned, cut off.

Secondly, the reason this was working was simple. The new 'word' didn't come from somewhere outside, it came from black peers.

Thirdly, the Brown Berets did practically no work with boys already addicted; their whole effort lay in prevention.

And lastly, it seemed to be working. While addiction spread in a mathematical progression in the suburbs, our own records at Teen Challenge showed a decline in boys coming to us from the ghetto.

So now it was 2:00 a.m. again, and I was once more at my Trysting Place in prayer.

'I see it clearly, Lord. I even think I see what You want me to do. Learn from the Brown Berets. Get the kids *themselves* to pass the word about drugs. Become an Apostle of Prevention.'

But then came that sinking feeling I was so familiar with.

This was easy to see as a goal, quite another thing to

realise. Who were the kids who could spearhead a counter thrust?

'Where are they, Lord? Show me, and I will then turn to this as the next main effort of my life.'

It was only a few days later that the invitation came to hold a rally in Phoenix, Arizona. As usual I placed it on my desk along with some others and prayed. Often nothing at all happened, and I was learning to accept No as readily as to accept Yes.

Well, on this occasion the invitation from Phoenix had that peculiar 'illuminated' quality I had come to recognise. It seemed brighter than the others around it. I never quite got over being surprised at this form of guidance. So far, not once had I been wrong in interpreting it.

'And this time, Lord? Do You want me to fly out to Phoenix?'

'There's someone I want you to meet there,' the Lord seemed to be saying.

So a little later I found myself in Arizona, wondering what encounter the Lord was preparing.

The meeting, I thought, was an exciting one. There was one dramatic moment when a young Baptist preacher asked if he could share the microphone for a minute. He told the audience how a few years ago, he started to do research in the occult. He bought Tarot cards and ouija boards, looked into witchcraft. Before long the interest became an involvement. In the end he left the ministry and began quite literally to worship the devil. Here to-night, he said, he wanted to confess what he had done, and to warn others against dabbling with the occult. There's no way to describe the effect he had on the audience. Scores of young people came forward to renounce 'the devil and all his works' and to turn to the Lord. Dozens more came forward with their bottles and pills and drugs and needles to throw them on the platform, declaring them to be part of Satan's world.

All in all, it seemed to me to be a good meeting, one of the best. The only problem was I still did not feel I had met the person I was supposed to meet in Phoenix. But since there was nothing much more I could say or do, I decided to dismiss the meeting.

But just then an attractive young teenage girl got out of her chair and walked slowly down the centre aisle. She came up to the platform.

'Mr. Wilkerson, may I please say a word?'

Well . . . after all the Lord had brought me here for some special reason which I had not yet found . . .

'Of course.'

What this young lady said has changed my entire ministry.

There was nothing hostile, nothing belligerent about this charming teenager. Yet the words dug into me as knives.

'Mr. Wilkerson,' she spoke into the microphone, 'you have been talking about drug abuse, homosexuality, alcoholism, devil worship. All these big hangups. I thank God for the kids who have been released from bondage.

'But, Mr. Wilkerson, you sure did miss me. And if you missed me, I think you may have missed hundreds of others here. We don't smoke pot, let alone stick needles into our arms. We don't drink. We are not homosexuals. And we hate the devil. We do have problems, all right. Sometimes they stymie us and keep us from standing up to be counted. But our problems, Mr. Wilkerson, seem so insignificant compared to these massive hangups that we just don't dare bring them out. If you want to know the truth, we really feel like forgotten teenagers.'

The young lady turned to me and smiled. I could see tears sparkling in the spotlights. 'I'm sorry, Mr. Wilkerson, that I had to bring this up. I just thought you ought to know how a great many of us feel.'

With that she went back to her seat. I was stunned. The girl had been so sincere. She was speaking for herself but I sensed she was also speaking for a large group of other young people.

About all I could do that night was to thank her for her honesty and say that I promised to take her words very, very seriously indeed. Then I dismissed the meeting.

That night back in my motel room I couldn't sleep. I felt certain that this message from a Forgotten Teenager, was the reason I had been brought to Phoenix. These were the young people who were to act as Apostles of Prevention, peer talking to peer, teenager to teenager. Their mission was incredibly important. They would be able, one day, to put a quiet pressure on their own age group: it wasn't cool to use drugs. I remembered a young girl who once told me that she had lied to her friends, saying that she was on heroin when she didn't even know how to use the drug. She confessed her reason: the kids on drugs got all the attention, it was the 'in' thing. Well, somehow, with careful attention to the Lord's leading, we were going to change all that.

A few days later I appeared on the Art Linkletter show. I found myself speaking a little too glibly about this new idea.

'David,' Art said, 'suppose you had to choose one best

solution to drugs in the suburbs. What would that solution be?'

'The job is for the young people themselves,' I said easily. 'Teenager to teenager, peer to peer. And I know who can do the job to. The Forgotten Teenager. Those kids out there who are clean, who are square, who don't use drugs and aren't involved in earth-shaking hangups. This is my mandate from the Lord now to harness the power of these great kids.'

Art didn't say anything except a sort of general Good Luck. But after the show he put his finger on something I hadn't seen yet.

'I haven't noticed these Forgotten Teenagers of yours making themselves heard before, David. What makes you think they'll suddenly become voices in the wilderness?'

And I had to admit he was right. As I thought about my supposed new mandate, I realised that there was one part of the speech given by my Forgotten Teenager in Phoenix which I had glossed over. What had she said? Something about problems that stymied her and kept her from standing up to be counted?

Yes, that was surely at the heart of the matter. Whatever these problems were, they were used by Satan to block effective action on the part of young people. I could just see it. They felt guilty about certain deeds and emotions and thoughts. How could they take a stand without being hypocritical?

So my *very* first task was to discover what these crippling teenage problems were, and to treat them with the same urgency as, say, addiction. With a blush I remembered that my own daughter Bonnie had once taken a problem to her grandfather rather than to me, 'because Dad's awfully busy with people's important hangups'.

'Lord,' I prayed, remembering Bonnie, 'I confess that I haven't placed enough stress on the troubles of our average healthy young people.

'What *are* their problems, Lord? Show me how to find out, please, so we can set these kids free in Your name.'

8

The Forgotten Teenager

Releasing the extraordinary power of . . .

I WAS QUITE CERTAIN now that my little sabbatical was
over. Not that life for me would become complex again,
involved with the administration of our programme: I
was steadily turning over more and more of the running
of Teen Challenge to my brother Don who has a flair for
administration. My work from now on out, I knew, was
going to be of a different sort. I could glimpse the extent
of the new horrifying problem of drugs in the suburbs.
Our old strategies and tactics were just incapable of meeting a situation where we have one youngster addicted today and two thousand tomorrow.

No, we had to break new ground. We had to listen
carefully to the Lord's own plan for battle, and in listening
I thought I heard again and again what I had said to Art
Linkletter. The teenagers themselves, if we could just
release their strangled power, were the most positive
force available for the battle.

But as Art had suggested, the trick was helping the
young person over his roadblocks so that his energies
were free. To do this we needed first to discover what the
Forgotten Teenagers' problems were and to see what
could be done about them.

I began making my way towards this Forgotten

Teenager by starting each of my crusades, now with a bold statement.

'Let me just say something loud and clear. I want to give a million hallelujahs for every straight kid in this place. I want to give a thousand thank-you's for those of you who are strong enough to say, "You can have your drugs, I don't need them."'

I was amazed at the response. Many times the whole auditorium would stand and cheer these young people. 'We're watching the beginning of a change,' I said.

But praising the Forgotten Teenager was not enough. Something was still throttling him. When we could get this out of the way these same youngsters would be able to stand before their peers and state their position.

So now for months on end during the final minutes of each rally, I was involved with a survey. Scores of thousands of teenagers answered the little questionnaire we passed out, asking for anonymous replies. The question I was most interested in was this:

What is your Number One Problem?

As we gathered in these replies, several of us at Teen Challenge spent time in prayer, analysing the answers. What *were* the problems of our young people today? I'll never forget the night I took Gwen out to our favourite Italian restaurant and shared with her our findings.

'Well, David?' Gwen said.

'Here they are. A hundred thousand answers more or less, and they add up to three worries . . .'

'Come on. Stop the drumrolls, honey.'

'First of all the kids are worried about the things they do that are wrong.'

'Sin,' said Gwen.

'Sin. Then, they want to get along better with other people, especially their parents.'

'Thou shalt love thy neighbour as thyself?'

'I hadn't thought of it that way. And then the last worry is about the future. What's going to happen to mankind? To the earth? How should we feel about the horrible news that hits us whenever we open the paper?'

'End times thinking,' said Gwen.

'That's what it is.'

'Those are the toughest problems there are, David,' Gwen said.

'I know, that's what scares me. The one thing I'm sure of is that I could never answer them myself. Would you pray with me about this?'

Gwen put her hand across the table and took mine. 'Of course.'

So right there before we lit into the antipasto and the pizza I prayed the prayer that was to launch me into the next phase of my work.

'Lord,' I said, 'I don't want to try to answer these problems out of my head. I want the answers to come straight from You. Please help me find a solution to the problems that are choking our Forgotten Teenagers.'

Over the next weeks and months I thought and prayed about the first set of problems: how to handle bad habits.

Just what were these habits the kids worried about? I got out the abstract of our findings and looked it over.

At the very top of the list were sexual concerns. Not the dramatic ones we dealt with at Teen Challenge, homosexuality and sadism and the like. The number one sexual concern of the Forgotten Teenager was masturbation. I suppose masturbation has plagued every generation. I know it bothers the young people of today, especially the clean-cut kid who is making an effort *not* to go the excessive route. He seems to find the answer to his sexual drives in masturbation.

Slightly less frequently mentioned was petting, especially in drive-ins. And at the far end of the spectrum was intercourse itself. The teenagers were frank to talk about this. Intercourse was far more prevalent among our fine young people than I had imagined.

The second most frequently listed problem was drugs. Even among the admirable Forgotten Teenagers — kids who do not have real addictions to contend with — there was frequent experimentation with drugs. They played with marijuana, LSD, speed and on rare occasions even heroin. But by far the most frequently used drug was alcohol. Alcohol had respectability, expecially in groups who did not want to break from their parents. Their parents drank, they drank. Not infrequently by the time a youngster was in his late teens he knew he had a problem.

I was surprised how often cigarettes came up as a major source of concern for the Forgotten Teenagers. They knew and believed the Surgeon General's reports. Yet somehow they had gotten started on tobacco and now could not stop. We who had been dealing with addictions of a truly horrible nature were tempted perhaps to overlook the guilt and the bondage that can stem from a cigarette. But when I read these kids' own statements, I no longer felt that way. Tobacco was a tool used by Satan to keep our young people from being free. As long as they were hooked on any drug, even nicotine, they felt hypocritical about taking a stand on grass, acid or speed.

'Lord,' I prayed early one morning when this really

became clear to me. 'I want to find out how You would tackle this problem — bad habits. I am going to stay here until You show me, please, what we should do.'

As soon as I had prayed this I remembered an interesting conversation with my mother. For years Mother has had a coffee house ministry in Greenwich Village where she is affectionately called 'The Village Square'. In her work Mother has met many homosexuals. 'I once kept a record,' Mother told me in the conversation I was now remembering, 'of how many homosexual kids really wanted to be released. And you know, David, only two per cent ever said clearly, "Yes, I want out." This is why we can't help much. Most of the homosexuals just don't want help.'

In contrast to this attitude was the attitude of Sonny Arguinzoni and my own brother Jerry. Each of them found a key which could be of real value to our own Forgotten Teenagers. For in Sonny's life and in Jerry's, *desperation* proved to be the real secret of change. As long as they did not really want to change, there was no real opportunity for God to work in their lives. They simply kept one foot on earth, one foot in heaven, and their split position made it impossible to move freely. However, once they became really desperate they were ready to hear the Lord.

So the first thing the Lord showed me about breaking bad habits was the same Desperation Principle I had discovered with Sonny and Jerry. I would have to ask, point-blank, 'Do you really want out?' If the answer is no at least the young person has now been square with himself. I do not want to stop masturbating. I do not want to give up drinking. I don't want to quit smoking.

But if the answer is yes, the Lord is equally anxious to help. And here the Lord showed me a second principle: if we really want to break a habit we should not try for victory by ourselves.

How often had the kids told me of their efforts to break bad habits. They had fasted, prayed, promised, chastised themselves, vowed to turn over a new leaf, devised a dozen ways to keep themselves from the source of their troubles. And yet more often than not they fell back. They just didn't have the resources, any more than an adult does. 'My sins have overwhelmed me,' says King David. The kids are not stronger than King David; on his own he was powerless before sin, as are we all.

So the Lord was teaching me a radical-sounding second lesson: If you want to break a habit, don't try for a victory; don't make any more promises, for promises are just another way of reaching for victory all by ourselves. Instead, and this was the last principle the Lord showed me, Expect a Miracle. Simply trust Jesus to bring freedom.

Well, these were the three releasing principles that the Lord gave me that night.

> Admit that you are desperate
> Don't try for victory by yourself.
> Expect a miracle.

I started to bring these principles to our Forgotten Teenagers and discovered time after time that they really did work. The third principle — Expect a Miracle — was the most fun to watch. We discovered that there were usually two ways in which the miracle was performed. Either the Lord mystically took away the desire itself, as he did with the boy who finally stopped smoking. Or else he brings about a change of circumstances.

For instance there was the young girl who told me of a love affair with a boy who had been arrested on a drugs charge. 'My father,' she told me, 'has forbidden me to see the boy again. I do want to obey my father. But you see we are having sex together and I just can't seem to break away. I've tried standing in front of the mirror and saying to myself, "I hate him. I hate him. I hate him!" But the moment I walk away I find myself saying, "I love him."'

So we looked at the three releasing principles. 'It seems to me,' I said, 'that you have met two of the criteria. You say that you are desperate, and you say that you know you cannot change by yourself. All that's left now is to trust Jesus to do a new thing for you. Expect a miracle! Will you try that?'

'Yes, sir.'

'Write me, will you? Tell me what happens.'

Three months later I had a letter from this young lady. Two weeks after I had talked with her, a strange thing happened. The boy's father was transferred to Northern Canada. The boy, Ron, was given permission by his parole board to go along. He said goodbye to his/my young friend, promising to pick up his life with her soon. However, when it came time for him to keep his promise he found that he was in trouble. If he left his father's custody he was liable to arrest. It was stay put or go back to jail.

'So you see, Mr. Wilkerson,' the girl said, 'the Lord *did* change the circumstances for me. Ron could not come across the border. I found that I missed him desperately for the first few weeks. But then I discovered the amazing truth that the thing between us was dying. And now I can report quite honestly that it is absolutely dead.'

It was exciting to watch. Time and again we heard similar stories of the Lord's work in the lives of young people, helping them to change.

So this was the first of the major problems facing our Forgotten Teenagers: how can I overcome bad habits? As I began teaching the three releasing principles I got reports by the hundreds and eventually by the thousands that the principles really do work.

Helping kids to break their old sin patterns, then, was the first great adventure I had in releasing the stymied power of the Forgotten Teenager.

The second adventure was to help heal broken relationships. The kids knew that there were bad relationships in their lives, and that the rankling and bitterness stood between them and freedom.

What could we do to help?

Since by far the greatest friction point was with parents, I decided to concentrate my work in this area. I admit that I was astonished at how virulent these negative feelings were. At one crusade a boy stated that he hated his father. I was surprised at the word. Could this be accurate? I decided to find out what other kids would say.

'How many of you,' I said to the group of young people in the auditorium, 'would say that you *hate* your parents?'

I couldn't believe what I was seeing. Almost forty per cent raised their hands. Perhaps they had not heard me correctly.

'I'm not talking about a bitterness between you and your parents, I mean do you *hate*?'

Only one or two put their hands down.

While I was recovering, one of the boys walked to the microphone. 'I think I can speak for a lot of us,' he said. 'Maybe hate is too strong a word, but I don't think so. Hate is when you boil up inside all the time. And that's the way my old man makes me feel. Just to see him walk into the room makes me churn. Isn't that hate?' Then he paused. He was having difficulty talking. 'But Mr. Wilkerson,' he said, 'I want to change all that. I want to love my folks again. Maybe there's a way . . .'

Well, this was an eye-opener. I had to get to the bottom of it. Over the next few months I asked the same question over and over again: *Why* do you have so much trouble with your parents? The answers tended to fall into groups represented by the following replies:

My parents are phonies, they say one thing and live another.

My parents don't try to understand me.

All Dad thinks about is his business.

Mom and Dad are always fighting.

Dad cheats and thinks nobody knows.

My folks drink too much.

My old man walked out on my mom three years ago and I hate the ground he walks on.

My people are too rigid in their standards.

The folks are always riding me about my clothes.

Well, there was no doubt that this deep negative emotion which the kids called hate was crippling our Forgotten Teenager. If we were ever going to watch him turn into a dynamic force we would have to help him get rid of that stumbling block.

Once again I took to my Trysting Place. I asked the Lord how our team could help. And slowly there emerged these key ideas:

First of all, just as we can depend on a miracle to break bad habits, so we can expect a supernatural help in breaking the bondage of hatred. Doesn't the Bible promise just such a new relationship? 'And he shall turn the heart of the fathers to the children, and the heart of the children to their fathers . . .' (Malachi 4:6).

It is often at one of our crusades that the first step of this miracle begins. A youngster takes that long walk down the aisle and gives his heart to the Lord and right there change begins. He is ready to love.

What happens then? After each of our meetings we hold special counselling sessions in which we tell the kids that *they* are different now but that things aren't yet going to be different at home. They can't expect their parents to take a first step. They themselves must be the first to bring a thaw to the winter that has ruled their home, for they are the ones now who can bring Christ into the situation.

Often when a young person carries out these instructions the results are touching and beautiful. One boy told me a story that gripped my heart. He had not, he said, talked to his mother for over two years. But after the miracle he found that he just couldn't hate his mother any more. He ran home intending to tell her he loved her.

'There Mom was, sitting on the living-room sofa watching TV and knitting,' the boy said. 'She looked so old and tired. I wanted to talk to her but there was this barrier between us. I started to walk back and forth there in the living-room. I think Mom must have thought I was angry, because she kept glancing at me without turning her head. Then, very nervous like, I sat down on the edge of the sofa next to her. All I wanted to say was "I'm sorry!" But I just could not. Finally — I guess it was the Lord — I knew what to do. I placed my hand on her shoulder and said one simple thing, "You're okay, Mom." Well, you should have seen my mother jump up and hug me.

"That's the loveliest thing I've ever heard," she said. Mr. Wilkerson, I've just got to report that it ain't half bad. I've got a good mother and it's going to work out okay.'

But the results are not always this encouraging. We've found that simply to send a teenager home full of love and compassion is often not enough. The change is too sudden for the parents to accept. Another boy told me a far more typical story of his experience when he went home. He too wanted to tell his mother that he was sorry and that he wanted things to be different. He managed to blurt the message out. His mother didn't even look up from the pot she was scrubbing. 'Aw, you've just been drinking,' was her only comment.

So when we send a youngster home now we have prepared him for a rebuff. We tell him it's going to take time to mend old hurts. We tell him he may have to act out what he is trying to say rather than state it in words. Do the dishes, we suggest. Take out the garbage. Clean your room. Just be nice to the folks. It's these actions which will speak when words cannot.

Then comes the next stage in the process of healing. Very often — most often in fact — the changes that have been taking place in the teenager are contagious. Parents begin to change too. And it is precisely here that trouble can occur and, if we're not prepared for it, spoil everything. For somehow or other our young people have never been taught a basic fact: parents are people. They are full of strengths and weaknesses. The kids need to *let the parents fail*. They need to realise that the parents are not going to be perfect. When it comes to expectations, there has to be plenty of breathing room between a kid and his parents. If this is allowed for, and if Christ is kept alive in the family, then it happens that the miracle comes to maturity.

We have found that these same principles, although most important when applied to parent–child relationships, are also helpful in healing broken relationships between brother and brother, a young person and his friends, kids and teachers. And as they are applied, it has been most encouraging to watch the kids come out from the shells that had been restraining them, into the powerful, dynamic and often Christian selves they were intended to be.

So. The first two great problems of our Forgotten Teenager were:

How can I cope with destructive habits? and,
How can I get along better with others?

The third of the great concerns was *What's going to happen to mankind?* I was astounded at the age level of the kids who saw this as their Number One Problem. They were often in their very early teens. Worry about tomorrow hung over them like smog, leaving them generally depressed.

They often just gave up. I'll never forget a visit with a friend in Wheaton, Illinois, which resulted in meeting his thirteen-year-old son Bobby. I would have said that Bobby was one of the Forgotten Teenagers — a clean-cut, attractive young Christian. I found myself wondering how he might define his Number One Problem. As it turned out, he told me. Bobby was afraid for the future.

'Mr. Wilkerson,' he said to me, 'I'm going to run away.'
'Oh?'

'Yes, I'm just going to bag it at school. There's no point in trying to relate to a world that's going to blow itself up soon. Things are out of hand, Mr. Wilkerson. There are forces too big to control and they've been let loose. The schools aren't helping us to look at these things. School is just a big box where you learn to turn your mind off. So I'm quitting.'

What could I say? Bobby seemed to be looking at his world with clear vision. I told him I sympathised with him, but I knew this wasn't enough. Bobby and thousands like him were reading every day about ecological disaster, germ warfare, atomic destruction, over-population. There was not much I could say to help him live dynamically under the threat of a dozen Damocles swords.

But then I saw that I wasn't playing fair with Bobby. Because as far as I *personally* was concerned I had an answer. I saw the present calamities with quite a special eye. For every day when I opened the newspapers and read of a new Middle East crisis, or of earthquakes in Peru, or of an exploding divorce rate I knew that I was reading about events which had been predicted thousands of years ago. And which were all vitally significant. For I saw these events as signs that Jesus was coming soon. Very shortly, I felt, I would have my most treasured dream come true: I would be living with Jesus, after His Second Coming.

How unfair it was of me not to share this with Bobby. Having a Jesus-centred interpretation of the headlines affected my daily life and I wasn't saying so.

But the minute I started thinking along these lines I realised that I was in an almost impossibly difficult area. How could I talk to a thirteen-year-old about so complicated a subject as the End Times. There were as many interpretations of the Second Coming as there were Christians, it seemed to me. The minute I tried to explain the End Times to kids like Bobby I would surely step on someone's theological toes. Besides, how could I possibly discuss Jesus' coming without using all those specialised, shop-talk terms. Pre-millennial, post-millennial, first appearance, second appearance, tribulation, Armageddon No . . . I'd never be able . . .

Bobby's face came before me.

Was I just going to leave him with his worries? There was real danger for him if I did. For without Christian insight Bobby could easily turn to the dangerous counterfeits of God's truth: spiritualism, clairvoyance, fortunetelling, false prophecy, anything that would attempt to interpret and cope with the overwhelming events of today.

So in the end I decided to write a letter to Bobby, explaining in terms a thirteen-year-old could understand what the Second Coming was all about, and why it was so important. I knew that I would be expressing just one theological view, but at least it is a classic one, held by many traditional Spirit-anointed churches.

This then was my Letter to Bobby about the Second Coming:

Dear Bobby,

When I met you several weeks ago I was really challenged by our conversation. Do you remember it? You said that as you looked around, you could see that mankind was going to kill itself off. You also said that even though you were a Christian you were going to quit school. There wasn't any point carrying on under present circumstances, and besides school was just a box where they taught you to turn your mind off: at school you weren't allowed to talk about the end of the world.

Well, Bobby, I'm writing you this letter in the hope that as a Christian you *won't* turn your mind off, and that what I have to say will encourage you to stay in there fighting. For there is so much for you to do! And there is so little time!

Bobby, the point is this. You and I both see the real probability that the world as we know it is coming to an end. For you this produces hopelessness. But for me, this produces hope. Because as I see it 'this world' needs to end in order for a fantastic new earth to be born. You know how often something . . . like a seed, for example . . . has to appear to die and be buried before a new birth can take place? Well, according to the Bible the same is true of the earth itself.

From what you have told me you have, up until now, been frozen by what you see going on. I hope that will no longer be true, my friend, for one crucial reason:

Not everybody is going to make it into this New Earth that is coming. The world's population will soon be divided between those who get to live with Jesus and those who have to go through hell.

Does that seem harsh? Before you make up your mind, I want to take a few moments to explain to you what I understand the Bible to say about these days immediately ahead. Then we'll come back to you and to your own personal role in this whole picture.

Just a word about Scripture. As a rule, when people explore this subject, they riddle their talk with long and sometimes difficult-to-grasp Bible passages. Which is understandable, because a lot of us are betting our very lives on those passages and they need to be accurate. The only problem is that for someone like yourself, just beginning to think about the world's coming to an end, these Bible passages can become so confusing you just give up.

So in this introductory letter I am going to do something different. I'm going to talk to you about what is called the End Times — the end of the world as you and I now know it — in modern everyday language. I'll use a few Bible passages in key places, but mostly, Bobby, I'll give you just the Scripture reference backing up what I tell you. I suggest that you read through this letter once or twice without ever going to your Bible to check me out. Then as you become familiar with the broad outline, go to each of the references, and read for yourself what Scripture has to say about these days we are in.

So, do you want to begin then?

Let's start with the basic difference between the view you expressed the other day and the view the Bible takes about the End Times. The difference is that you see the world as simply coming to an end with some horrible disaster. The Christian who believes in the Second Coming agrees, in part. He lives in this same time zone, the same warning signs, but for him there is one dazzling, incredible event that will happen *before* the world goes to hell.

Before that horrible destruction, Jesus is coming again.

This Second Coming is going to be quite a different scene from the baby-in-the-manger story. This time Jesus will come in glory and in power (Luke 21:27). He'll come quite suddenly, in a fraction second, no longer than it takes to blink an eye (I Cor. 15:52). There will be a rallying call like a trumpet sounding (I Cor. 15:52).

The very first thing that will happen when Jesus calls is

for a great separation process to begin. Please read this part carefully because it is crucial to understanding why you just can't drop out now.

There will be two separations. First, the separation will take place among all the people who have died. Because everyone, the Bible says, will be resurrected at Jesus' Second Coming (John 5:28). The guys who have done good will be separated from those who have done evil, the one headed for life and the other, I'm afraid to say, for damnation (John 5:29). So people like Hitler didn't get away with it by committing suicide. He'll get up from his grave on the day of Jesus' Second Coming to face his judgment.

And what about those of us who are not dead but who are alive at the Second Coming? We'll go through a separation, too, Bobby. Some people will be singled out for very special and favourable treatment, and others will be left behind to go through the worst tribulation the world has ever seen. The Bible puts this vividly. 'Then shall two be in the field; the one shall be taken, and the other left. Two women shall be grinding at the mill; the one shall be taken, and the other left.' (Matt. 24:40-41).

What is this special favourable treatment? Where will the fortunate ones be taken? The most amazing thing will happen. The Christians — the real, believing Christian who has Jesus alive in his heart — the Christian will suddenly be caught up in a cloud and taken to meet the Lord (I Thes. 4:17).

Pretty fantastic?

I should say so. For one thing, Bobby, think of the chaos this is going to cause. A lot of cars will be driverless. Announcers on the air will simply disappear. Many pilots on jet liners will find themselves without a co-pilot: the co-pilot will be with Jesus. Another reason this is going to be pretty fantastic is that those people who go to Jesus know a kind of happiness they've only glimpsed here on earth. One of the old words used to describe this state is 'rapture'. Like being totally in love and totally loved all at the same time. We will be given new bodies that are immortal (I Cor. 15:53).

Now let's get back to something I said a while back. Isn't it pretty gross having a lot of people in a state of rapture while the rest of mankind is back there having a hard go of it during the great *Tribulation*? Yes, the Tribulation is going to be gross. But it isn't that God has been unfair, for He gave everyone plenty of warning. He has told us how to know that He is about to come. Whole books have been written on the subject of these signs of His Coming, but if you want to make some preliminary notes so you can warn your friends (are you beginning to see why none of us Christians can drop out now?) I'll give you what seem to me to be most important ones. Jesus called many of these, 'The beginning of sorrows'. Before Jesus comes again, we have been warned:

There will be a return of the Jews to Palestine from their dispersion (Ezekiel 36:24).

There will be great stress, outbreaks of violence, a breakdown of order (2 Timothy 3:1–4)

There will be a world-wide spiritual awakening among the youth (Joel 2:28).

Then there will be a yearning for peace and security lulling the world into complacency (I Thes. 5:3).

There will be a 'business as usual' attitude similar to the times of Noah (Matt 24:37-39.)

There will be earthquakes, famines, plagues (Matt. 24:7).

There will be a Mid East crisis (Ezekiel 38:8, 9).

There will be a lack of expectancy about the Second Coming. Unbelief about His return will be characteristic of the times. (II Peter 3:4).

Among the Believers, however, there will be a growing excitement in the inner man prompted by the Holy Spirit that the return is imminent. (Luke 21:28).

There will be an outbreak of homosexual mass murders — similar to the lawlessness in Sodom (Luke 17:28-30).

In times past people have believed that the end was at hand. What makes us think we are right while they were wrong? In the past some — but not all — of these criteria had been met. Jesus, when He spoke of the timing of His Coming referred to the signs and then said, 'Verily I say unto you, This generation shall not pass, till all these things be fulfilled' (Matt. 24:34). The way I see it, Bobby, 'this generation' means the generation in which *all* of the signs are pointing in precisely the same direction. When 'this generation' comes, then Jesus says the Second Coming is at hand. Read over the list again. How close are we today? Isn't it really possible that the end is upon us, and that there is very, very little time left before the great separation will take place, some going to be with Jesus and the rest going into the terrible Tribulation?

Let's go on a bit about that Tribulation. This is a period when the worst fears of mankind will all be realised. Up until the Tribulation the Holy Spirit had been active on earth, restraining evil (2 Thes. 2:7). But now He no longer takes this restraining role (although as we'll see in a moment He will still be at work leading the Jewish nation to Jesus). Without the Spirit's braking efforts and with no real Christians around any more to bring stability to society, things get pretty horrendous.

Evil will reign. Man's fleshly ways will be allowed to go rampant. He will live by his passions and lusts. 'For men shall be lovers of their own selves, covetous, boasters, proud, blasphemers, disobedient to parents, unthankful, unholy, without natural affection, trucebreakers, false accusers, incontinent, fierce, despisers of those that are good, traitors, heady, highminded, lovers of pleasures more than lovers of God: having a form of godliness, but denying the power thereof' (2 Timothy 3:1-6).

This will be an incredible time of terror too. There will be a continuation of the famines and plagues and earthquakes which began as signs of His coming (Matt. 24:7). And above all there will be one final cataclismic war called Armageddon. For out of a ten-nation block (Daniel 7:23-25) which was set up just before His coming, a super czar will arise gaining a reputation as a peace maker (Daniel 11:21, 24). He will woo Israel and will eventually move his headquarters to Jerusalem. (Daniel 11:45). And there he is going to double-cross the Jews and set himself up as God (Daniel 9:27).

All the while a gigantic army has been building up in Asia. It will be the largest ever seen: 200 million strong (Revelation 9:16). It will come towards the Mid-East through Pakistan: the Euphrates River will be dried up so as to allow the army to march across it (Revelation 16:12). These hordes will descend on Israel and the final conflict, Armageddon, will commence at a place called the Valley of Jehoshaphat (Joel 3:2). This place really exists, Bobby; I have been there.

As Israel then turns to the battle of Armageddon, God will intervene and rain down fire from heaven (Ezekiel 38:22). This will perhaps be a limited thermo-nuclear war. But in all events, it will be a swift affair, something like the Six Day War between Israel and the Arab nations. The slaughter will be so great that Israel will spend months just burying her dead. (Ezekiel 39:12). But in spite of this, Israel will survive as a nation. There will be a remnant of 144,000 Jews who will live through the Tribulation (Revelation 7:4-8). These are the Israelis who will be led by the Holy Spirit to have an encounter with Jesus, so that, at last the nation of Israel will recognise Him as the Messiah.

The end of human history will come about at that time, Bobby. The break between God and man, which began with Adam, has now been healed. Jesus at this point makes still one more literal physical appearance. To distinguish this from his Second Coming it is usually referred to as the Day of the Lord. Jesus in person now sets up the New Heaven and the New Earth (Revelation 21:1) which will be enjoyed by all His saints.

This New Earth where Jesus will reign will be as uniquely beautiful a time as the Tribulation was horrible. The Tribulation lasted seven years but the reign of Christ on earth will last a thousand (Revelation 20:3). Satan will be out of the picture altogether (Revelation 20:3). There will be perfect knowledge (Isaiah 11:9). Men will live so long that 100 years will just be the beginning of a lifespan (Isaiah 65:20). The wolf will lay down with the lamb (Isaiah 11:6). Disease and death and tears will be removed. 'And God shall wipe away all tears from their eyes; and there shall be no more death, neither sorrows, nor crying, neither shall there be any more pain: for the former things are passed away' (Revelation 21:4).

And finally after the thousand years of peace with Jesus ruling there will come the eternal reign of God (Revelation 21:3).

Well, Bobby, that's the outline of my understanding of the End Times, and believe me, I've only hit the high spots. Some of the points I have made are open to a different interpretation of course, since we draw on hundreds of widely scattered and sometimes obscure Bible references; but by and large I believe it is fair to say that the view I have expressed represents one of the great traditional interpretations.

I do hope that by now you see why a young Christian like yourself should not drop out of the battle. For it depends on you, and others like you, to spread the word so that as many people as possible end up on the happy side of the equation when the great separation comes. There is much you can do, Bobby, to help your generation — and mine too.

What should you do? Help me to raise up a Get-Ready Generation, Bobby. The Bible says that there are three things we should be doing if we are to be ready for His Coming:

First of all we should be *watching*. 'Watch therefore: for ye know not what hour your Lord doth come' (Matt. 24:42).

Then we should be looking for His coming. 'Looking for that blessed hope, and the glorious appearing of the great God and our Saviour Jesus Christ' (Titus 2:13).

Then we should be *expecting* the coming. Jesus will appear to all of his people who are expecting His arrival.

'. . . and unto them that look for Him shall He appear the second time . . .' (Hebrews 9:28b).

These are the key words: watch, look, expect. If we follow them, Bobby, we shall be ready. We can be in an attitude of rejoicing. Each new crisis can be viewed as another gate into a new world *if* we are among the ones who have made the basic decision to be on the Lord's side. How terribly important it is to tell as many people as possible this good news!

Well, that was my letter to Bobby. Later I shared the thoughts with thousands of other kids. I found that young people like him everywhere responded with enthusiasm to the simple presentation of these truths. Released from hopelessness they have picked up the same divine obsession that so many adults feel: go out and teach and preach the Second Coming.

Exactly how soon will the Second Coming be? Jesus said that not even He knew the hour (Mark 13:32). The precise minute is not ours to try to divine. But we are to be ready throughout a span of time. And we are to watch those signs! They are everywhere. When they all point in the same direction . . .

Once recently I stood near a group of long-haired, blue-jeaned, shoeless and attractive young Jesus People on the West Coast as they were being interviewed by a hostile reporter. He was questioning them about their life style. For he saw in them simply people who had been hippies and who were still hippies, although now they were living in what they call a 'Jesus house', a commune for Christ.

'The thing I want to know is this,' the reporter said. 'What's going to happen fifteen years from now when you kids are a little older and are running things in the world.'

The kids smiled. 'Mister,' one of them said, 'that's just not a real question for us. Because we don't think we'll *be* here fifteen years from now.'

'What do you mean?'

'We're in the End Times, Mister.'

'Is that good or bad?'

'It depends on where you are in Jesus, sir,' a girl said. 'It's a sad-glad story. For anybody who is into Jesus, and is expecting His return — it's a glad story. For people who are not — it's really a sad one.'

That's the message I began to bring to the young people who were worried about the future. All that is happening is part of a sad-glad story. If we are into Jesus, as the kids say, and are expecting His return, then we know for sure that it is a glad story. So the most important thing we can do with our time today is preach, witness, work to bring as many possible into the right side of that equation.

So. The kids gave me three top priority problems. First they were worried about cleaning up their lives. Then they were worried about getting along with others. And finally — most important of the three it seems to me — they were worried about the world's tomorrow.

As I and the team that with me came to grips with these problems and attempted to bring answers that would release the Forgotten Teenager, we began, rather dramatically, to see the very changes we had dreamed of. We have watched him stand up and say, 'I don't use drugs because I don't need them. And I don't think it's cool at all. I don't have far out sexual hangups and I'm sorry for anybody who has to use sex to be popular.'

But most amazing of all the Forgotten Teenager has, once he sensed his new freedom in the Spirit, done far more than take a stand *against* something; I have watched him start to be most dynamic in taking his stand *for* Jesus.

This, of course, is headline material all over the country now, as it took shape from many different sources of which we are only one: it is what we call the Jesus Movement.

The Jesus Movement among young people was the thrust God said would come. It's an amazing thing to me to see the power and thrust of these kids sweep across the country. Now it is sweeping overseas, finding sharp persecution in countries where materialism or political thought is threatened.

So this is how the Lord is leading us in our new mandate.

It is exhilarating. And one might think that with such important work to do the Lord would see to it that we had no *personal* problems in the Wilkerson family which might slow up or threaten the work.

Unfortunately, this was far from true.

9

The Fear I Couldn't Conquer

Maybe you too have this problem . . .

Throughout all these long hard months I continued trying to be careful that we avoid becoming a huge institution. My brother Don picked up more and more of the organisational work of Teen Challenge in New York, while Gwen and I concentrated on the Forgotten Teenager and his cousins in the Jesus Movement. I was now in an 'encouragement ministry', encouraging young people all over the country to recognise their own potential.

And this in itself created a problem so huge that for a while it looked capable of scuttling everything we were trying to do.

For my new ministry required a great deal of flying. In fact I was clocking nearly 100,000 miles a year, travelling not only across the United States and Canada but also to Europe, Africa and South America.

Which I would have enjoyed except that I continued to hate flying. Well, no, that's not quite accurate. I was *afraid* to fly. I'm what's known as a white knuckle flyer. I constantly look out the window to make sure the wings are not falling off. When fire comes out the engines, no one can persuade me that that is normal. The mere sight of the cockpit terrifies me, for I am certain that no human could master all those controls.

But the thing which I fear worst is turbulence. Once that plane starts bouncing up and down, my knuckles turn white as I grip the seat arms, my stomach knots, and I know for sure there is nothing — nothing — I can do to keep the fear down.

I guess I've tried every technique known, spiritual and temporal. I've tried praying, fasting, relinquishment, seeking deliverance, requesting intercession. On the plane itself I turn to the guy next to me — poor fellow — and start to preach at him the very minute the plane takes its first bounce. Perhaps a good old-fashioned sermon will take my mind off the rocking aircraft.

When none of these approaches seemed to temper my fear I turned to the boot-strap method. I'd conquer that fear by my own effort! Not a very sound idea, but I was desperate. Once, for instance, a friend suggested that I take flying lessons. That way I'd learn what a plane could and could not do. It made sense; after all, flying statistics were greatly in favour of a safe trip: I'll find out why.

So the next time our team went on a trip and I had a bit of spare time, I went out to the local airfield for a lesson.

My first time up the instructor told me to put my head between my knees and to describe my sensations.

'What are you feeling?' the instructor asked.

'Dead panic.' Silence from the instructor. 'I'm praying if you want to know!'

More silence from the instructor. Then he said in a defeated tone, 'I just wanted to show you what a cloud bank is like. When you can't see, it feels like you are falling. Would you tell me, Mister, why you want to learn to fly an aircraft?'

'If you want to know, it's because I'm petrified.'

That instructor took me back to the field and wouldn't go up with me again.

On my fifth lesson a different instructor told me to put the plane into a stall. 'Pull the stick back and head straight into the sky until you stall,' the instructor said.

I liked the idea! Now I would learn what a plane could do! I pulled back the stick just as the pilot had said. The little craft nosed upward, upward, upward and then suddenly it began to shiver and to slide backward on its own tail.

I passed out.

That instructor too refused to go up with me again.

But with sheer gumption (and by using instructors who did not know each other) I finally did manage to complete the course. It was now only a matter of getting a physical. We were in Phoenix, Arizona, I remember. I went to a doctor recommended by the instructor, filled out my application and gave it to the nurse. When the time came she called me in.

There was the doctor in a wheelchair.

'I see that you are a clergyman,' he said, looking at the application. 'Tell me something, why do you want to fly? Are you planning to be a missionary to Africa or something?'

When I told him the truth he just looked at me stonily. 'I'm not going to pass you. Take a look at me. I was studying to be a missionary in Africa myself as a matter of fact. Medicine. I thought I'd better learn to fly. One day my plane fell into a tree. I'm not going to let you take your life into your hands just to try to get rid of a fear. Besides your eyes are bad.'

So I never got my licence and over the years my fear of flying grew worse. Our schedule called for a crusade on nearly every weekend. Let's say that we had to fly out of New York on a Friday. By Thursday I was tense. I would stay up very late praying and occasionally listening to the weather reports. Then the next day, bleary-eyed and fear-racked, I would take off for some distant city. Next week I would have to go through the patter all over again.

It didn't help much when a genuine air crisis arose. Once Gwen and I had just taken off from Los Angeles, headed for Tulsa. We had reached 18,000 feet when I heard a sudden whistling sound! The plane wobbled. It felt to me as if it were plunging. I grabbed Gwen's arm. 'The plane is falling!'

'No,' Gwen said calmly, 'that's just your old fear.'

But Gwen was wrong. The captain came on the intercom with a message about not getting excited. But it seemed we had a little problem. The rear engine was on fire. 'But don't be nervous,' the captain said, 'there's every reason to believe we can make an emergency landing.'

When we got back to Los Angeles we were cleared for an immediate landing. The foam trucks were out. Ambulances stood by. We made it. When we got out I looked back and saw that the entire rear end of the plane was charred black.

When we got into the waiting-room, I collapsed into a chair. 'How can I go on flying, Gwen?'

'Maybe you're supposed to quit, honey.'

But how could that be. I had this mandate from the Lord . . .

Then two weeks later it happened all over again. This time we were headed towards Tampa. At 25,000 feet the pilot began to talk about 'a bit of weather ahead'. By a bit of weather he meant a hurricane.

The pilot — bless him anyhow — kept filling us in on terrible details. The hurricane was over the Tampa area, but it looked like we were well within the flying limits there. We could land quite safely. Doubtless.

So the pilot decided to give it a try.

We started to come down. The plane shook and creaked. Women screamed. The stewardesses were white-faced and kept tightening their seatbelts.

We literally *bounced* into Tampa. With a screeching of brakes and burning of rubber, the plane hit the runway, the flaps were thrown up, engines were reversed, and as the plane wobbled to taxi-speed, the pilot came on with a casual comment, 'Sorry about that, folks. A bit rough there.'

As if flying weren't bad enough I now found that I had not one, but two fears to contend with, and they were related. For I was sure my fear of flying had produced an ulcer in me. My stomach hurt constantly. I found myself reliving my father's last illness. How I recalled his screaming. How I lived through the day Dad was wheeled out to the ambulance and sirened to the hospital. He almost bled to death before life-saving blood transfusions could be administered.

In spite of many clear-cut periods of recovery through prayer, Dad finally died of his ulcer. I promised myself that I would never, never subject my own family to the throes of such an attack. I drank milk and gulped something the doctor gave me, and watched my diet but one day as I was coming down the stairs at home I passed out. I too was rushed to the hospital just as Dad had been. I too was put into intensive care. The X-rays showed a duodenal ulcer. It was in the same place my father's ulcer had been.

The doctors, however, felt that with proper medication and correct eating I would be able to contain the ulcer without having to undergo an operation. I was pleased. But now I *knew* I had to conquer my fear of flying. I had to conquer it not only for my own sake but because I knew it didn't help others much. Here I was talking about the miracles I had seen the Lord perform, delivering people from addiction to heroin, say, and I could not get victory over my own fear. As a matter of fact things grew steadily worse. I began snapping at my staff. I especially did not want them to talk about white knuckle flying. Once I heard an old friend on the staff say 'Let's be sure to pray for the Chief on this flight.'

I became angry. 'Don't worry about me,' I said testily. 'Pay attention to your own problems.'

And of course in time I grew angry at God for not setting me free. 'Is that too much to ask!' I demanded during my prayer, in a tone and attitude which I hope was due to my discomfort.

Then, one day on a flight out of Chicago I was going through my usual pains and fears when I discovered that aboard the aircraft was an old friend and fellow pastor, Dr. C. M. Ward.

'Do you mind if I sit next to you?' I asked. I had a little feeling that somehow I might be able to borrow confidence from this stalwart Christian.

'Delighted,' Dr. Ward said. We visited for a while and then he began to read! Very calmly, too. The trip was choppy, but that didn't bother him at all. In time I found the courage to talk with him about the troubles I was facing.

'Here we are bouncing along in this crazy manner, and I seem to be the only one bothered by it. All the other passengers just take their booze and sleep. But I'm so tensed up my stomach hurts again.' C. M. Ward looked at me steadily. 'You don't seem disturbed,' I rushed on while I had the courage. 'What's your secret? I've fasted and prayed and ... My faith just doesn't work here. It's not much of a witness, is it?'

C. M. Ward was too much of a gentleman to answer that one. But he did ask me if I were afraid of dying. I thought a while.

'No. Not of dying. I remember all those times on the street when kids would threaten my life, and I wasn't afraid. No, it's more like a fear of falling. Something ancient within me that I *cannot* dissolve.'

'There you are, then,' said C. M. Ward. 'You have a structural weakness.'

'A what?'

Dr. Ward put down his book and turned towards me. 'Have you ever noticed that when I am on a platform I never sit between two people? I'll tell you the reason. I have a terrible form of claustrophobia. Even to be *that* close to being shut in fills me with panic.

'I've prayed about it and fasted too, just as you are doing. And nothing happened. Maybe our problem is close to Paul's 'thorn in the flesh'. There are certain weaknesses which we are never going to be delivered from. I call them structural weaknesses.'

Well, that was a new thought to me, that we could have structural weaknesses which we never *would* get around. It was helpful, but it did not get rid of the pain in my stomach. I did not know that God, through C. M. Ward, had planted in my mind the seeds of a solution which was to surprise me.

The solution did not come about right away. It took still another crisis to shake me loose from conventional thinking so that I could hear what God was saying.

One day we were on Vancouver Island in British Columbia. There were two ways we could go back. One was by ferryboat, the other by air.

'I think we should take the boat back,' I said.

'Oh, oh,' said Dallas Holm, our soloist. 'That's bad news. I get seasick.'

'Besides,' said our Crusade Director, Dave Patterson, 'it's a two-hour trip by sea and a half-hour by plane.'

We ended up taking a little commercial puddle jumper. The minute we were airborne I knew I had made a mistake. For we flew into a bad storm. We kept trying to find the right altitude. Up and down, and down. And up. It was like riding a bucking bronco. I could feel that plane slap the clouds. Lightning flashed all around us. My stomach was torn in two.

To make matters worse, there was a man across the way eating bananas, one after one. Didn't he realise what danger we were in? And a lumberjack in front of us was stuffing homemade bologna sandwiches into his mouth. Didn't he realise he should be praying!

But all of a sudden even these cool passengers were in trouble. For without warning our little plane fell 1,000 feet. A stewardess was walking down the aisle carrying cokes. The plastic glasses and the Coca-Cola flew all over the cabin, mixed with bananas and bologna sandwiches.

Women screamed. Babies cried. The stewardess recovered herself and began to mutter apologies.

And then by a miracle equal to any in the Bible we landed in Seattle. Right away we had to board another plane. And another rough flight. By the time we reached home I was again holding my stomach in pain.

'Gentlemen,' I said to David and Dallas, 'that does it. Except for times when we absolutely *have* to fly, you'll never, never find me in the air again.'

I didn't need to argue. 'Okay, Chief, we won't question you any more,' said Dave Patterson. 'That *was* pretty bad.'

Bad enough in fact that it triggered a new attack from my ulcer. I called the doctor and as soon as he examined me he started talking about an operation. It all happened so quickly. Before I knew it I was being wheeled into the operating-room. As I came to, I was praying in the Spirit. In the recovery-room, the Lord dropped a scripture verse into my mind. 'There hath no temptation taken you but such as is common to man: but God is faithful, who will not suffer you to be tempted above that ye are able: but will with the temptation also make a way to escape, that ye may be able to bear it' (I Cor. 10:13).

What a promise this was! God was speaking so clearly. When we face testings we cannot overcome, He plans a way of escape for us so that we might be able to bear it. As I lay there in the recovery-room I suddenly *knew* the way of escape the Lord had planned for me. It was as unorthodox as it was simple. I had been bound to a cultural idea that today you did your travelling by air. How ridiculous. From now on, I didn't care how they laughed, *I* was travelling by bus!

By bus! But right away I started to argue against the

thought. Here we were living on one coast and a lot of our work was on the other coast: we would have to spend most of our time on the road.

'Move to Dallas.' The words seemed to be dropped so clearly into my mind. Was it the Lord? 'Your staff will stick by you. I did not call you to *places*, David, but to *people*. I would like you to move to Dallas.'

When Gwen came to see me a little later I told her. 'Honey, guess what? We're moving. To Dallas. I'm going to travel by bus from now on out.'

Gwen just laughed. 'Well!' she said. 'If you want a confirmation, I already knew something was about to happen. In fact, I've been getting the children ready. "Expect Daddy to make a decision that will affect our lives," I told them. So this is it. We're moving to Dallas and you'll be travelling by bus. Well, all I have to say is, Praise the Lord!'

As soon as we were able to move, Gwen and I drove to Dallas to explore the land. I still had lingering doubts about whether we were making the right decision. So I tried a new experiment. I would not put a fleece before the Lord, but I would ask Him for a *token of goodness*. I picked this up from the 86th Psalm, where David said, 'Shew me token for good; that they which hate me may see it, and be ashamed: because thou, Lord, hast holpen me and comforted me' (Psalm 86:17).

And the Lord surely did that. I asked Him for a token that we were going in the right direction. And He sent me to a very special builder. I picked his name out of the classifieds. 'Come in,' the advertisement said.

So I did. When I walked in the builder was sitting behind his desk shuffling papers. I handed him my card, and was immediately embarrassed at his enthusiasm.

'You have no idea how many years I've been waiting to meet you, David Wilkerson. Let me know what I can do.'

So that same afternoon we sat down with architects and sketched out the floor plan for an office.

'When would you like to get started?' the builder asked.

'Well, I'll have to raise the money first. I am going to need money for a bus and for the building.'

The builder helped me here too by introducing me at the bank.

That same afternoon I had a credit line of $75,000. I was committed to a building and to a bus, without a penny of down-payment. The Lord had given me not only one but two tokens of His goodness.

Looking back over this whole experience I see now that nothing but good has come out of it. In reshuffling our schedule, we are able to work it out to have six days on the road and ten at home. This is considerably more than we had before. Now we are able to stop the bus, get out and exercise. We can come and go when we want to without depending on airline schedules. And for the first time I'm able to see America. We can carry our literature right with us on these trips, and interestingly we save more than fifty per cent on travel costs.

Frankly, the fear of flying is still with me, but who cares. Every now and then I must take an aeroplane, as when we went to Europe. I know by looking at my knuckles that I'm just as scared as ever. But at least it is a once in a while experience.

Many, many of us are built with structural weaknesses which we are not to conquer. Paul says they are there to keep us humble. When we face these, admit our inability ever to overcome them, He will — if we just ask Him — make a way of escape that we may be able to bear it.

But there was one more *personal* problem the Wilkerson family had to face, a problem that was far more devastating than the fear of flying. I want to share this with you here at the very end of this book because I think it is *that* important.

10

Work Out Your Marriage With Fear and Trembling

Perhaps for every husband and wife there comes a particular time when you have to. . .

CHRISTIANS NEVER GET DIVORCES.

Christian marriages are made in heaven, and of course the little squabbles a believing husband and wife may occasionally encounter are easily patched up.

I've heard these clichés all my life; and all my life I've known that there is a gap between what I hear people say and what I see them do. I'm afraid an awful lot of my Christian friends do get divorces; and I'm afraid that Christian home lives are often filled with problems that are just not talked about. There is a rule of silence about such troubles in the home.

Well, Gwen and I want to make an exception to this rule of silence. As the ministry of Teen Challenge developed, Gwen and I began to encounter difficulties beyond imagining in our own marriage.

We have prayed about this carefully, together, and we have decided to risk being frank. Because we believe that we have come through the major testing of our marriage with something to say to other couples facing similar difficulties.

It happens that the trouble in our house stemmed from

a physical problem which affected our emotional lives. I don't suppose there is any better way to proceed than to start way back at the beginning, when we were still living on Staten Island, in New York . . .

Cancer is something you always *hear* about without ever believing that it can strike your own family. This is especially true when you are young, and when you are trying desperately to live in the centre of God's will. He would just never let anything like that happen.

Still, there was that lump on Gwen's side.

We decided to go to the family doctor out on Staten Island and ask him about it. He was reassuring.

'I believe that all we have here is a swollen ovary,' he said. 'Happens frequently with women. Doubtless nothing to be worried about. But keep in touch.'

We left his office reassured.

But then the pains began. They must have been intense, for more than once when Gwen did not know I was watching I saw her grab her side. She never said a word. Gwen is the opposite of a hypochondriac, she never wants people to know how bad things are. During these early days of our problem — before we began to suffer emotionally — Gwen's condition pulled us closer together. I hurt with her. I tried to comfort her in as many ways as possible such as, for example, taking extra vacations whenever I could arrange it.

On one such occasion, when we were on our way to Pittsburgh to visit her mother, Gwen finally admitted to me that she knew something was very seriously wrong. 'I just can't stand it any longer, honey,' she said. 'I wake up in the middle of the night biting my tongue to keep from screaming.'

As soon as we got to Pittsburgh we made arrangements to see a specialist. He examined Gwen carefully then took me into a private room where he gave me a summary command.

'Get this young lady into hospital.' He started filling out some papers. 'I want your doctor in New York to call me. Quick now. Maybe there's still time.'

This was when I made the first of a series of mistakes. Sins, I should call them now, although at the time I thought I was acting correctly. Gwen and I had always been as honest with each other as we knew how, yet now I found myself playing games.

'For my peace and for yours,' I said to Gwen, trying to sound casual, 'I think maybe we'd better get home. I've had enough vacation, anyhow. We probably ought to slip you into the hospital for a couple of days so we can really find out what's causing this pain.'

Gwen looked at me and smiled. She played the game too. 'I could use a good rest,' she said. 'I have the strangest kind of tiredness. It's like my strength is oozing out of me, like I'm losing my life force.'

Two days later we were in the Staten Island General Hospital. Gwen was X-rayed and had a barium enema. The following morning I was at the office in New York interviewing a drug addict. My secretary stepped in and interrupted.

'Your doctor is on the line,' she whispered to me. 'He said to tell you it's a matter of some urgency.'

I know the blood drained from me for I felt light-headed. The addict looked at me in alarm. 'You all right, Mister?'

'Yes. All right, thank you. But we'll have to let you see someone else, if that's okay. My wife's got . . .'

I still couldn't bring myself to use the word. I picked up the phone, heard from the doctor that he wanted to see me right away. I gathered up my things and said a quick goodbye and ran out to the back courtyard where my motor-scooter was waiting. I'm sure I broke all records that day for driving through the city to the Staten Island ferry.

Now, in the family doctor's office my eyes met the eyes of a tired and defeated man.

'Mr. Wilkerson, I'm sorry,' the doctor said. 'I missed it.'

I was angry. 'What do you mean, missed it!'

'I'm sorry. We doctors do make mistakes, you know. It is almost certainly cancer. We need to get into surgery immediately.'

So then and there we began the awful arrangements. Once again I played games with Gwen. 'The doctor thinks maybe you should go to the hospital for some further tests,' I said.

'"Some further tests." That is his way of saying cancer, isn't it, Dave?'

I turned away.

From my Trysting Place prayer-room out in the garage I got on the phone. I called close friends who, each in turn, got on the phone with his close friends and we backed Gwen up with as much intercession as we could muster.

I knew it helped too. A few hours later, we were in the hospital. Gwen was putting on her gown. She had a peace about her that could only have come from the support prayers. Still, we couldn't look each other in the face and have a good cry. We couldn't say, 'Well, honey, this is it.' We just could not bring ourselves to face the world of cancer.

Gwen crawled up on to the high hospital bed. She leaned back. 'I'm so tired, Dave.'

Two surgeons came in. They called me into the hall. One held an X-ray. 'Mr. Wilkerson,' he said, 'a growth the size of a lemon has attached itself to the junction of the bowel. We are going to go in tomorrow to see what we can do.'

The doctors moved off down the corridor mumbling surgery-talk to each other. I stood there in the echoing hall, immobilised. Then I went to the fountain and had a drink of water. Then I asked a nurse for the correct time. Then I looked at a bulletin board.

'Wait a moment, David Wilkerson!' I said just under my breath as I foot-dragged my way back to Gwen's room. 'What's happening? You're not walking in the Light.'

Walking in the Light. What a wonderful phrase. Its imagery was so clear: the Christian must walk in the full, searching, honest light that comes from the Lord. And neither Gwen nor I — but especially I — had been willing to risk that.

Just then our family doctor came back down the corridor. I stopped him.

'Doctor,' I said, my hand on his arm. 'I want to tell Gwen the truth. Will you help me?'

'Well it's about time,' the doctor said. 'It's much better knowing.'

So together we went in and told Gwen. In simple lay talk the doctor explained what was happening and what must be done. He said that tomorrow we were going to see if we couldn't take care of the situation once and for all.

The doctor left. Gwen looked at me and smiled. 'Well, dear . . .'

And at last it came. The breaking and the tears. The honesty. We had waited so long for this. How much better it would have been if from the beginning we had looked into the eyes of the Lord and trusted.

We were making progress, but I was still not able to pray for Gwen with faith. It was Satan's trick, I am sure. I could pray with faith for addicts but could not pray for Gwen.

But here too the Lord did not leave us stranded. For there in that sterile hospital room Gwen and I realised another break-through. It was *Gwen* who encouraged me.

'Honey,' Gwen said, 'I've known all along that it was cancer. And I have a word from the Lord. He has told me that He is going to give us a very special kind of faith. He called it the faith of Shadrach. When Shadrach, Meshach and Abednego were looking into the fiery furnace they knew that God *could* deliver them, but if He did not, they would trust anyhow. That's going to be our faith, David.'

So, holding hands, at last we had the prayer that had been so long in coming. We prayed for the faith of Shadrach. 'As we face our own fiery ordeal. Lord,' we said, 'we ask for the kind of faith that trusts, no matter what happens. Thank You ahead of time for granting this request. Thank You very much indeed.'

The next day I was back at the hospital early to watch as Gwen was wheeled into the operating-room. Surgery took an hour longer than expected. I sat in the waiting-room going over again and again in my mind the story of the fiery furnace, drawing from it comfort and courage.

Finally the surgeon came through the swinging doors into the waiting-room. He still wore his green gown and cap. In his eyes was the same look of weary defeat I had seen on our family doctor's face and I remember wondering if perhaps all doctors felt this way when confronted with cancer.

'What a shame,' said the surgeon, sitting down in front of me. 'Cancer is such an ugly thing.'

I was ready to die. 'What's the news, Doctor?'

'Just what we thought, only there was more of it. We cut out everything we could find. Now all we can do is wait.'

With that he got up and walked away, shaking his head.

I took a long walk, trying to gather courage to go back upstairs. When I did go in they were just wheeling Gwen over to the recovery-room. She was barely conscious. She opened her eyes and saw me.

'Did they get it all out, honey?'

I told her what the doctor had said. 'They believe it's all gone, honey. With luck it's no more pain. With luck we're home free.'

Gwen closed her eyes. 'We'll see,' was all she said.

So in our marriage we had two new tools, which shortly we were to need desperately: the faith of Shadrach and a new understanding about the importance of honesty. As if to underline the honesty, the surgeon later took us into his office and gave us a little speech.

'You folks are ministers of the gospel,' he said. 'And yet on this subject of cancer you keep cheating. Now I don't want you to do this any more. I want you to face your trial as honestly as you can, especially with your friends and your family. Use the word "cancer" not a substitute. Don't shrink from it. Here I am a medical man talking to you about honesty, I'm sorry. But I know from experience that it makes a big difference.'

So we went home, and we did talk frankly about our troubles. Gwen recuperated rapidly. We went back to making plans for ourselves. After a year we were sure that we were indeed 'home free'.

Then one day as Gwen and I were working in the yard this strange tiredness quite suddenly overcame her again. She sat down on a lawnchair and called to me.

'Dave, I'm awfully tired all of a sudden.'

Oh no, I said to myself. Here we go again! For this was that different tiredness that both Gwen and I knew by now. I guess everyone who has had a growth in his body has experienced it. It is something almost spiritual, mysterious.

We didn't delay. We took Gwen back to the surgeon immediately. He examined her and did find another swelling. 'We'd better get into the hospital right away,' the surgeon said.

This time, though, the report was much better. The lump was non-malignant. Still, both Gwen and I came through the experience shattered. Gwen expressed it for both of us.

'Do we have to live the rest of our lives in constant fear of cancer? Do we have to wonder when we will get hit again? Maybe once cancer is in your body you never do get better. Maybe it would be better if I just went to the Lord right now.'

I spoke sharply to Gwen. She shouldn't even be thinking like that. Gwen wept. Without realising it we had passed over a line. The physical battle was beginning to affect our emotions.

That first little run-in passed almost unnoticed. We went right on with our lives, even making major decisions that would reach into the future. One night Gwen and I were taking one of our nightly strolls. She took my hand. She said a strange thing:

'David,' she said. 'I want another baby.'

I was caught off guard. 'After two operations? Do you think you have the strength?'

But Gwen knew her mind. 'I want to feel like a woman again,' she said. 'I want to know that I'm not through.'

'Well, we'll talk it over with the doctor.'

So we had our planned baby. A year later little Greggy was born. He was a husky, rugged child. Gwen felt closer to that baby than all the rest, I think, because of all she'd been through.

Another year passed with Gwen in reasonably good health. She was active, especially with the baby. Then when Gregg was a year old Gwen went through the worst crisis yet.

It began with the same battle with weakness. We were in Memphis, Tennessee, when Gwen grabbed her side. 'I'm having another attack, honey.'

'How can you? That part of you is gone?'

'I don't know, but I sure know it hurts.'

We prayed and Gwen felt a little better but she admitted to me that she had been passing blood.

'I think we had better get home.'

We didn't get there before trouble exploded. Going down the Pennsylvania Turnpike, Gwen had yet another attack. We turned off into the nearest town. A doctor heard her history and examined her.

'I'm sorry,' he said. 'I wouldn't dare try anything here. All I can do is give you a sedative. But you'd better get back to New York as fast as you can.'

There, the news was the worst that we had yet heard. Gwen needed a radical hysterectomy. The surgeon used the same words he had used before. 'We should be able to get it out once and for all.'

So, my dear Gwen was back up on the operating-table. Again, the long hours of waiting for the results. Again, the helpless look as the surgeon gave his non-committal report. We'd wait and see.

Before we went home the doctor gave me a private warning. 'Mr. Wilkerson,' he said in his consulting-room, 'you should be prepared for radical changes in your wife's emotional life. She will experience feelings of rejection. She will be jealous. She will have spells of anger. And severe depression. You name it. It will help if you realise that this is all the result of physical change.'

At the time I didn't grasp what I was being told. I said to myself, 'I can rise above it. We have prayer support from hundreds of people. We've fought battles before. We'll come through this one okay, too.'

We very nearly did not come through.

The first expression of Gwen's depression took a strange form. She began to find that she had other things to do during our morning prayer time. She would only join me when I specifically asked her to. The place-keeper in her Bible stayed on the same page day after day. Whenever I tried to talk with her about what was happening she began to cry. It was the first encounter we had ever experienced of a vicious tool of Satan: he gets us into such a negative frame of mind that we will not turn to our one best source of help. 'Just leave me alone,' Gwen said.

At first we rode with these sessions of depression pretty well, I guess. If Gwen couldn't pray for herself, couldn't read the Bible, I'd have to act for her. And I did, too. I counted it a privilege to stay up an extra hour praying and absorbing the Word for Gwen.

But as the weeks dragged by my own lack of sleep, plus trying to carry on for both of us, touched off a stupid reaction. One evening when I brought Gwen her cup of coffee she said, simply, 'Not tonight.'

I stalked back to the kitchen angry in a new way. Not angry at Satan. Angry at Gwen. 'If she doesn't want me to help, I won't help,' I said, tossing the coffee down the sink like a pouting child.

And then I caught myself. What had the doctor said? This was part of Gwen's permanent condition. It was what we could expect.

It was precisely at this point that a new element began to enter our relationship. Fatigue. Both Gwen and I slowly grew tired of battling.

It was insidious. I could watch Gwen fighting the effects of her radical surgery. She got up in the morning reasonably fresh, fixed breakfast with a visible effort to be cheerful, and even started to sit with me during our Quiet Time, though admittedly out of a sense of obedience.

Then by lunch little irritations loomed huge with her. The telephone made her jump. She always sent someone else to answer the doorbell, to avoid contact with people.

By mid afternoon she was having a constant struggle to keep from snapping at anyone around her. I was home one Saturday afternoon when for the first time in my life I heard her scream at the children. She ran into the bedroom and called me to her. She pulled my sleeve. 'Honey, why did I do that? I don't know what's happening to me. I'm so frightened. Pray for me!'

Of course we prayed. We got right down on our knees beside the bed. But if I were to be devastatingly honest I'll admit that I prayed in the same hopeless mood I knew when I first learned Gwen had cancer. Then, and now, it seemed to me I could pray for others and not for my own.

And Gwen's Faith of Shadrach? Where was it now? That kind of trust was one thing when we were facing a crisis, a one-time fiery furnace; it seemed quite inadequate to us when we faced an ordeal that stretched relentlessly over the months.

And eventually over the years. For the slow erosion of our bulwark of defences took a long time. I fought as did Gwen with all of the tools I possessed at the time. The more we struggled, the weaker we grew. When, at last, jealousy came into the scene we were not prepared to tackle it.

How well I remember the night. We sat in the living-room. All the kids were asleep. We had, over the past hour been talking (well, 'talking' is too light a word). Gwen wished I could spend more time at home. I used the word teenager once too often: I had to keep faith with the young people. There were all those teenagers . . .

'David,' said Gwen, quietly, evenly, 'I've got to ask it. Is there a particular teenager?'

I was dumbfounded. But what in the world do you say to a question like that. I knew it was the onslaught of the suspicion our surgeon had predicted. But that did not ease the shock. Of course there was no particular teenager. While I was trying to come up with just the right way to state that to my Gwen at this awful moment in her life, she said something else.

'David,' her voice had that same calm levelness that was so devastating. 'You don't love me any more. You want to get away.'

It was a simple statement, the verbalisation of something that had been growing in her for a long time: I knew that. I got up from my chair and went over beside Gwen, and sat down. I tried to reassure her that I was stating the truth, that there was no one else in my affections, no thought of getting away. Gwen was not satisfied. Slowly she pulled her hand away from mine and said the same thing she had said in the hospital when I predicted so foolishly that we were 'home free.'

'We'll see, David. We'll see.'

Gwen got up and went to bed.

Now the terrifying thing is that Gwen's worry which ten minutes ago I had answered honestly in the negative, I could no longer answer with such confidence.

Get away?

The thought was planted in soil quite ready to receive it. Wouldn't it really be a kindness to Gwen herself: I was clearly the source of a great deal of emotional pain for her.

I snapped my mind shut on such thinking, and followed Gwen to bed. She was already sound asleep ... or at least she seemed to be asleep and I didn't investigate.

How insidious is Satan's work. I see all this as the devil's snare now. But at the time the solution of running away seemed alluring, with nothing of the ugliness of Satan about it.

Weeks passed. Now, every time we had a run-in I escaped into a fantasy. I'd draw a cheque from the bank and run off to Mexico. I wouldn't get a divorce, but suddenly I could understand people who did. I'd . . .

'David,' Gwen's voice interrupted my daydream, 'what *do* you think? Should Gary go to Day School?' And I had to admit I hadn't heard a word.

At first all serious efforts, both Gwen's and mine, to heal our marriage were interspersed with these fantasies; but in time this was reversed: the fantasies were interspersed with efforts to make the marriage work. And it was during one of these valiant-effort times that I came to the crisis which I shall never forget.

I had to go to the west coast for a banquet and rally. Because I thought it would be good for our marriage I asked Gwen to come along. It happened that I was scheduled for a trip overseas shortly afterwards and so I was carrying my passport and a rather large sum in traveller's cheques with me.

Gwen and I were upstairs at the hotel, dressing for the banquet.

I do not recall what the specific was that slid us into a quarrel on this night. It could have been anything. But I do know that suddenly there was a barrier between us, like an unclimbable wall.

Yet we had to go to the banquet. A while later we walked in. I tried to put a veneer of pleasantness over our arrival and over our meal. Gwen was more honest. We sat next to each other at the round table, said 'Amen' together to the blessing, passed each other the inevitable fruitcup and roast beef and green peas and all the while we did not even look at one another.

The banquet droned on. Suddenly I hated the routineness of banquets and rallies. Suddenly I hated the struggle with Gwen, trying to battle a situation which never yielded to our good will and trying. Suddenly I knew that I was going to bag it all.

I was actually going to leave. That very night I'd be in Mexico.

I pushed back my chair.

'Excuse me for a little while, will you?' Gwen did not look up.

I walked down the heavily carpeted corridor, through the lobby, out on to the boulevard and headed for the bus station. 'It'll just be for a little while,' I said to myself. I fingered the traveller's cheques in my pocket. 'I wonder how long I can live on this. If I choose some mountain village . . .'

Then I was at the depot. A sign announced the departure shortly of a bus for Mexico City. I sat down.

'I don't have the patience for it,' I said almost aloud. 'I've tried. I cannot get the victory.' I even remembered a Bible passage to help me in my determination to flee. '. . . Oh, that I had wings like a dove! For then would I fly away and be at rest. Lo, then would I wander far off, and remain in the wilderness. I would hasten my escape from the windy storm and tempest' (Psalm 55:6-8). That's what King David so much wanted to do. And so did I. I was just not man enough to cope. I knew that it was a physical problem with Gwen, and as things were going now, I was blowing the marriage. I had to get away and try to figure it all out.

Then, while I was mustering courage to approach the window the Lord spoke to me.

'David, you're a fool.'

I almost turned around, the voice was so clear. But I

knew instantly that this was no flesh and blood person speaking to me. This was the Lord.

'Yes, Lord?' I said under my breath. I sat down heavily, oblivious to the bus depot surroundings. The Lord then spoke to me again, so softly, so kindly, full of compassion and at the same time with a terrible vitality.

'What's happened, David? It's Gwen who is suffering from the operation, not you. Haven't I spoken often about the need to persevere. Don't tire, David, but come to Me.'

I got up from my bench and looked at my watch. There was just enough time. If I ran.

I ran. I looked neither to the right nor to the left as I dashed back through lobby and corridor and took my seat next to Gwen, to the nervous-smiled relief of our hosts. Gwen now looked at me. She gave me a tentative little smile too.

'Honey, I love you,' I whispered. The master of ceremonies was making a preamble speech about our interest in the Forgotten Teenager. I reached over and gave Gwen a kiss on the cheek, quite too long a kiss for a banquet. She felt soft and yielded.

That night I preached on Psalm 55:6-8. It was a sermon inspired by the Holy Spirit, I have no doubt, because I had planned to talk about something else. I listened as the Spirit spoke through my lips, talking to me—and to many others who were also just plain tired—about Christian stick-to-it-iveness. The Psalmist David expressed for us all the *longing* to flee, but David was the greatest of all Hebrew Kings precisely because he never gave up. He fell ... and got up again. He was discouraged ... and kept going. He understood what it was to want to quit ... and he hung in there. It was the power of God's love that kept him going. And that power was available to any one of us tonight if we refused to listen to the discouraging lies of Satan.

All through that sharing-time I was conscious of Gwen's face. It seemed to shine up at me. When I was finished and returned to our table Gwen whispered to me, 'I've never seen anything like it, David. The power of God shone through you. Now I know that somehow we're going to get through these battles.'

I whispered in her ear.

'You know what I would like to do?'

'What's that, honey?'

'Let's take another honeymoon.'

Two weeks later we drove towards the Mid-west, just, the two of us, on a good old-fashioned honeymoon. We got out pencil and paper and wrote down a set of guide-lines for our life with each other. They would not be rules, for we would end up using rules against each other. These would be more like mottoes which each of us separately would be responsible for. We have tried to follow them carefully ever since then. They've been so helpful, that I would like to jot them down for whatever value they might have for others.

1. First of all, we knew that we must try to *be honest with each other*. This was the big lesson the doctor had taught us. We must try to look at the disagreeable and frightening things that were upsetting us.

2. Let's remember that *there are priorities in our attach-ments*. Gwen reminded me that there were ways for her to feel jealous that had nothing to do with a female rival. She could feel threatened by my work, my own childhood

family, my friends (who often were different from 'our' friends).

'As far as deep emotional attachments go, David,' Gwen said, 'I'd like to know you turn to God first, then to me. In third place would come all the other claims on your attention. We're supposed to be honest: that's honestly how I feel.'

3. *Don't smother*. Now it was my turn to express a man's need, because I panicked at the thought of being smothered. And during Gwen's depression she tended to hold on to me with a quality that came close to smothering.

4. *Each should try to liberate the other*. We should give each other the maximum liberty possible. Gwen confided that she felt in a backwash. I was always meeting people, always being stimulated and challenged. 'Honey, my life is so incredibly small,' she said. 'It's about 400 square feet: from the garage, to the car, to the kitchen, to the bedroom. I talk with friends about silly little things in the supermarket when I really want to be challenged. I want work. Work that will not just keep my hands busy, but my heart busy, too.'

So we decided that Gwen should work with me at Teen Challenge.

She thought she would be good at answering the letters of needy people. So she took on the task of writing back to people who had confided their deepest troubles.

And on her part Gwen would liberate me by agreeing never, except in prayer, to question my goals. She would trust the 'leadings' of God in my life.

5. *We should expect problems*. We would have to get away from the king-and-queen-living-in-a-castle attitude and realise that outside was a whole courtyard of problems.

We would expect problems. We would not let the fact that there were problems throw us. Our attitude would be, 'Well, here comes problem 1,827. Problem 1,828 is right behind it.' We promised ourselves we would joke about problems. We would throw our phony idealism out the window, not fearing that just because we had problems we had lost some kind of early magic. Our Bible back-up here was 'Many are the afflictions of the righteous: but the Lord delivereth him out of them all' (Psalm 34:19).

6. *Never fall into the trap of saying that we don't understand each other.* This, I had noticed among my friends who were getting divorced, was the one most common phrase that kept coming up. Each man and woman felt that his wife or her husband did not understand. We weren't going to have this happen to us. If we felt really threatened by misunderstanding we promised that we would approach each other to talk it out.

7. *We would watch out for stab wounds that are too deep.* Little things that we had been saying to each other that hurt almost too much, from which there might not be recovery. Gwen, for instance, was hurt if ever I corrected her English in public. I had to promise not to do that again. She, on her side, when angry called me a hypocrite. I knew that there were parts of me that were phony. And I didn't want to be reminded about it.

8. *We were going to love each other tempestuously.* Physically. Gwen and I both laughed over the first visit we had to New York when a friend, Phil, met us in the taxi cab. I had warned her that some of the things Phil said might embarrass her. And Phil really did come straight to the point that night.

'Little Lady, I've got a piece of advice for you. David

has been called by God to work with prostitutes. He is going to be wined and dined and celebrated by people across the country. And he's going to be tempted.'

I shrivelled up inside.

But Phil went on. 'There's only one way to keep your man out of trouble, my dear. Love the life out of him. Every time he leaves the house make sure that his mind cannot possibly be thinking in another direction.'

Gwen laughed, but we both knew Phil was right. For a healthy marriage has to have a good allotment of sex whether the husband must be away a lot or not. We agreed now that this was one of the best pieces of advice we had ever had. We were going to keep the fire burning brightly, make sure that boredom never set in.

9. *Don't say 'I'm sorry' unless you really mean it*. We would never cut an argument short, saying that we were sorry simply to shut off the disagreement. Nor would we ever go to bed on our anger.

10. *Don't overlook the little things*. Gwen had a way of hanging her silks in the bathroom. It used to drive me nuts. I finally confessed this to her and she promised to be careful in the future. On my part, I apparently had a way of not being available when chores had to be done.

We promised not to allow these little things to mushroom, get out of hand. We would talk about them. And act upon them.

Well, that was it. We came back from our honeymoon, passed the place where we had spent our original honeymoon twenty years earlier.

'You know where we are?' Gwen asked.

'Of course I do.'

'It was pretty awful, wasn't it? The original honeymoon I mean,' Gwen said. And we both started to laugh uncontrollably.

'What about this one?' I asked Gwen.

She reached over and hugged me tightly.

'This one, my dear, is a thousand thousand times better.'

Epilogue

IF SOMEONE WERE to ask me which part of this book I thought to be the most important, I know what my answer would be.

And it is a different answer from the one I'd have given when I started writing *Beyond the Cross and the Switchblade*, eighteen months ago.

For over the past year and a half we have had another war in the Middle East, the energy crisis is upon us, persecution of Christians is taking place in such odd places as Uganda. More and more we see signs of the End Times approaching. I have been asked to make a separate book out of the Letter to Bobby, so important is this subject.

I am doing that but I am leaving the Letter in this book too since it is such a large part of what I want to say to young people. I have also produced a movie about the End Times, *The Road to Armageddon*. It is by far the most ambitious project World Challenge has undertaken. If you would like to learn how your church can share a print of the movie, why not drop me a line.

David Wilkerson Youth Crusades
P.O Box 38344,
Dallas, Texas 75238.

In the meanwhile Gwen and I both urge you, as a part of the Body of Christ living in the most exciting time ever, to remember one thing. Remember what our attitude should be, every time we read in the headlines of some new sign of His coming. We should *rejoice*. The End Times means the end of the bad times and the beginning of something great. All these turmoils, tumults and tribulations are going somewhere. They are going towards our union with Jesus.

There could be no better news than that.

David and Gwen Wilkerson
Dallas, Texas